The Triumph of God's Sovereignty

By
JOHN C. WHITCOMB

MOODY PRESS
CHICAGO

All Scripture quotations, except those noted otherwise, are
from the *New American Standard Bible,* © 1960, 1962, 1963,
1968, 1971, 1972, 1973, 1975, and 1977 by The Lockman
Foundation, and are used by permission.

The use of selected references from various versions of the
Bible in this publication does not necessarily imply publisher
endorsement of the versions in their entirety.

The author wishes to thank the following journals and publishers for permission to use material and quotations: *Andrews University Seminary Studies;
The Biblical Archaeologist; Biblical Research;* Doubleday and Company, Inc.,
for ESTHER *(Anchor Bible),* translated and edited by Carey A. Moore, copyright © 1971 by Doubleday and Company, Inc., reprinted by permission of the
publisher; *Journal of Biblical Literature* 95 (1976) 43-58; *Near East Archaeological Society Bulletin;* and the Oriental Institute, University of Chicago.

Library of Congress Cataloging in Publication Data

Whitcomb, John Clement, 1924-
   Esther, the triumph of God's sovereignty.
   Bibliography: p. 127.
   1. Bible. O.T. Esther—Commentaries. I. Title.

BS1375.3.W47   222'.9'077   79-12756

ISBN 0-8024-2016-8

CONTENTS

ILLUSTRATIONS

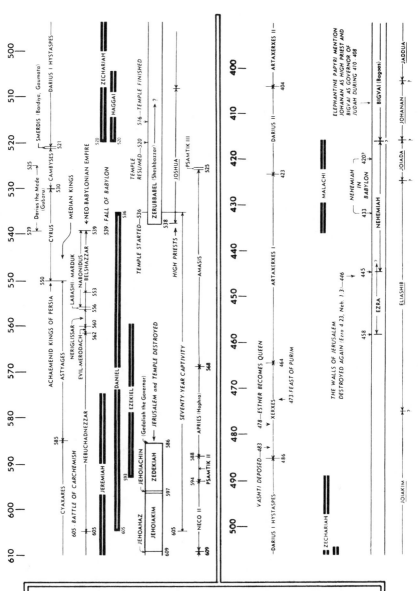

CHART OF OLD TESTAMENT KINGS AND PROPHETS (610-400 B.C.)

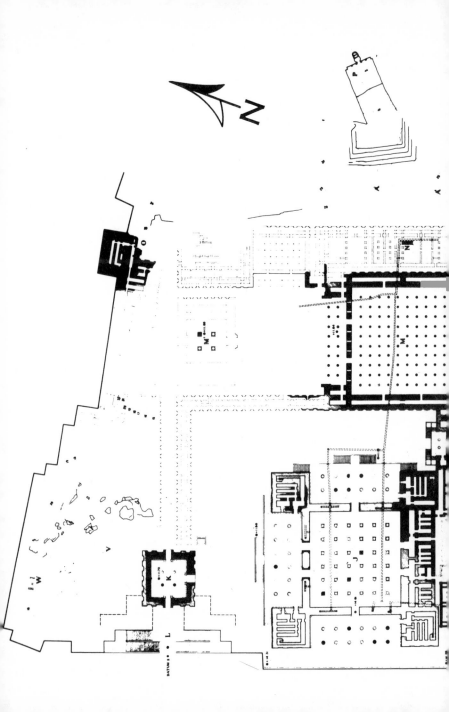

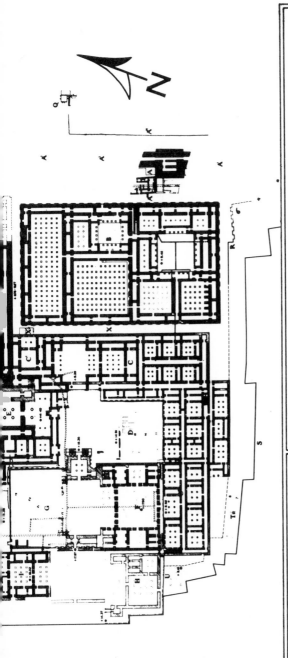

PLAN OF THE TERRACE OF PERSEPOLIS

A   EASTERN FORTIFICATION, GARRISON
A'   EASTERN TOWER MOUNDS
A'' RETAINING WALL
A''' GARRISON STREET
B   TREASURY
C   RESTORED MAIN WING OF HAREM
C'   SERVICE QUARTERS OF HAREM
C'' WEST WING OF HAREM
D   PALACE D
E   COUNCIL HALL
F   PALACE OF XERXES
G   PALACE G
H   PALACE H
I   PALACE OF DARIUS I
J   APADANA
K   GATE OF XERXES

L   TERRACE STAIRWAY
M   THRONE HALL
M'   UNFINISHED GATE
M'' NORTHERN FORTIFICATION
N   STAIRWAY TO DRAINAGE TUNNEL
O   NORTHERN FORTIFICATION
P   TOMB OF ARTAXERXES II OR III
Q   CISTERN
R   SOUTHERN FORTIFICATION
S   FOUNDATION INSCRIPTION OF DARIUS I
T   DRAINAGE OUTLET
U   POST-ACHAEMENID PAVILION?
V   UNFINISHED COLUMN DRUM
W   POSTERN?
X   "HAREM STREET"
X'   SECONDARY ROOMS

Copyright 1953 by the University of Chicago

RECONSTRUCTED PLAN OF PERSEPOLIS TERRACE. ORIGINAL SURVEYS BY THE EXPEDITION ARCHITECTS (1930–39). ADDITIONS IN NORTHERN PART (*in broken lines, unshaded*) BY THE IRANIAN ANTIQUITY SERVICE. FINAL DRAWING BY A. R. HAUSER. SCALE, 1:1,000

Courtesy of the Oriental Institute, University of Chicago

CONTOUR INTERVAL ONE METER

ELEVATIONS IN METERS FROM DATUM

        EXISTING FEATURES
        RECONSTRUCTED FEATURES
        SUB-SURFACE FEATURES
        SURFACE DRAINS
        RECONSTRUCTED PARAPETS, BENCHES, ETC.
        ADDITIONS AFTER SURVEY BY IRANIAN ANTIQUITY SERVICE

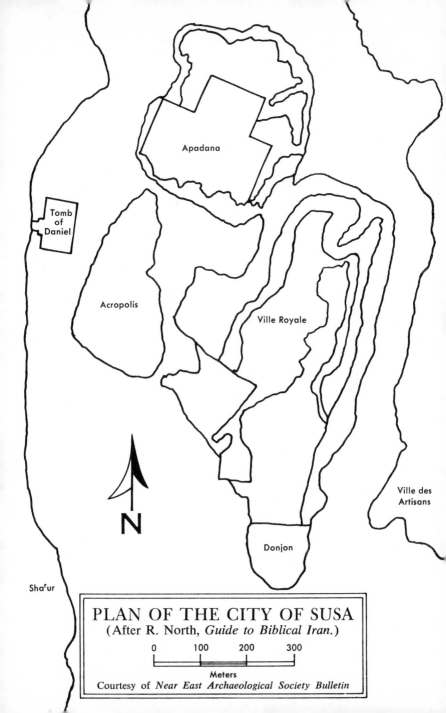

Apadana

Tomb
of
Daniel

Acropolis

Ville Royale

Ville des
Artisans

N

Donjon

Sha'ur

PLAN OF THE CITY OF SUSA
(After R. North, *Guide to Biblical Iran*.)

0   100   200   300

Meters
Courtesy of *Near East Archaeological Society Bulletin*

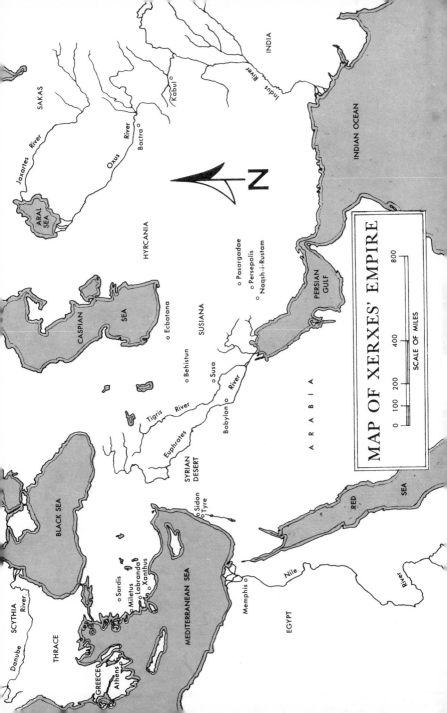

MAP OF XERXES' EMPIRE

SCALE OF MILES

0 100 200 400 800

To Norma,
my loving wife

ACKNOWLEDGMENTS

The author wishes to express special appreciation to the following individuals, who made valuable contributions to the preparation of this commentary:

Mr. Robert Ibach, Jr., librarian of Grace Theological Seminary, who researched various sources used in the book and proofread the final galley sheets.

Dr. John J. Davis, executive vice-president and professor of Old Testament and Hebrew, Grace Theological Seminary, who read the entire manuscript and made helpful suggestions.

Dr. Edwin Yamauchi, professor of history, Miami University, Oxford, Ohio, for recommending various technical studies on Medo-Persian history and for reading the final galley sheets.

Mr. Ronald L. Minton, postgraduate student at Grace Theological Seminary, for making various helpful suggestions on the original manuscript.

It has been a pleasure to work with Mr. David R. Douglass and Mr. William E. Henry of Moody Press. Their encouragement and helpful counsel in the preparation of the manuscript for publication have been deeply appreciated.

Finally, special thanks are due to Mrs. Betty Vulgamore, Mrs. Cathy Miller, and Mrs. Gail Glasscock, secretaries of the faculty, Grace Theological Seminary, who typed the manuscript; and to my dear wife, Norma, and our six children, whose prayerful encouragement made the entire project possible.

INTRODUCTION

THE BOOK OF ESTHER is a vitally important part of the body of Holy Scripture. Just as much as Deuteronomy, the Psalms, or Isaiah, it is inspired, inerrant, historically accurate, canonical, divinely authoritative, and theologically significant. To be sure, this is difficult for some Christians to understand, because the book contains no mention of God or religious activities and because it seems to focus on the mere physical survival of Jews at the expense of their Gentile enemies. Even worse, the hero (Mordecai) and the heroine (Esther) do not seem to be concerned for the laws or testimony of their God. How, then, can we assert that Esther is a vital part of Holy Scripture?

As the answers to these questions begin to unfold before our eyes, we shall discover truths about our God that are precious and otherwise unknowable. Especially encouraging to the believer is the relevance of this book to the status of the nation of Israel today. We serve and love a God who cannot lie and whose gracious purposes for the world, in spite of sin and Satan, cannot be defeated. It is with this expectation, therefore, and with the assurance that God the Holy Spirit will open the eyes of those who truly desire to know His truth (Ps. 119:18), that this study of the book of Esther is introduced.

AUTHORSHIP AND DATE

Just as we do not know who wrote 1 and 2 Kings, so also we do not know who the inspired author of the book of Esther was. But in spite of the efforts of some scholars to date the book down to the time of the Maccabean era, its Persian date is becoming more obvious upon closer inspection. Carey A. Moore, who denies the inspiration and full historicity of the book, nevertheless admits that "the narrative nucleus" of the book had to be written during the Persian period because (1) the Hebrew of the book is much earlier than that of second-century-B.C. Qumran literature, (2) there is a total absence of Greek vocabulary in the book, and (3) "the Hebrew of Esther is most like that of The Chronicler which is now being dated to ca. 400 B.C."[1] Furthermore, the sympathetic attitude in Esther toward a Gentile king "is quite possible for a Jewish writer in the Persian Period (539-332), but less appropriate in the Hellenistic Period (331-168), and highly unlikely in the Maccabean Period (167-135)."[2]

Students who are not conditioned by the presuppositions of negative higher criticism are free to look more closely at the detailed descriptions of the palace furnishings at Susa (cf. Est. 1:6-7; 7:8) and discern the authority of one who was present at the scene before this magnificent palace was destroyed (435 B.C.).

With regard to the author himself, one suggestion worth considering is that "the absence of reference to Jerusalem and the mention of the Jews 'scattered abroad and dispersed' (3:8) indicate that the author was himself one of the *Diaspora*. . . . The Persian words and knowledge of Persian customs that the book contains, suggest that its writer lived in Persia. . . . It is a plausible conjecture that the author was a Persian Jew who had come to live in Judea, and wished to commend the observance of Purim to the people of that land."[3]

1. Carey A. Moore, *Esther,* The Anchor Bible (Garden City, N.Y.: Doubleday, 1971), p. lvii.
2. Ibid., p. lx.
3. Lewis B. Paton, *Esther,* International Critical Commentary (New York: Scribner's, 1908), p. 63.

CANONICITY

Until recent days, it has been generally agreed by liberal critics that the book of Esther was not considered canonical until the so-called Council of Jamnia (A.D. 90). L. B. Paton, for example, claimed that in Palestine, as well as in Alexandria, "there was long opposition before it was admitted to the Canon,"[4] but that later Judaism sought to compensate for the opposition of her predecessors by praising the book in extravagant terms.

However, *the "Council of Jamnia" did not canonize Esther* or any other book of the Old Testament. It simply recognized what had already long since been canonized by God through the inspiration of the original text.[5] There is an important distinction between canonicity and theological understanding. Not everything in the inspired and canonical text of Scripture was understood or appreciated by every Jew. But it was not for that reason dropped from the Bible. The same issue faces the church in our day, as some theologians boldly assert error to exist in the original text of Scripture simply because it does not fit into their preconceived philosophical notions. Christ and the apostles did not handle the sacred Scripture in this manner.[6]

Old Testament scholars of liberal persuasion are now adopting a more moderate view of the matter. Carey A. Moore, for example, admits that Josephus (A.D. 37-100) considered the book to be canonical, for he recognized the antiquity of the book and paraphrased it in his *Antiquities of the Jews.* The oldest available list of Jewish canonical books also includes Esther (*Baraitha* in *Baba Bathra* 14b-15a, second century after Christ). Moore concludes: "Grounds for

4. Ibid., p. 97.
5. Cf. R. Laird Harris, *Inspiration and Canonicity of the Bible* (Grand Rapids: Zondervan, 1969), p. 155, and R. K. Harrison, *Introduction to the Old Testament* (Grand Rapids: Eerdmans, 1969), pp. 277-79.
6. Cf. Harold Lindsell, *The Battle for the Bible* (Grand Rapids: Zondervan, 1976).

the book's claim to canonicity at Jamnia are easily surmised: (1) the book claimed to be an accurate historical account of a time when the Jews were saved from almost certain extinction, and (2) the book provided the *raison d'etre* for a popular religious festival. Moreover, by the time of the Council of Jamnia the Jews, with Jerusalem destroyed by the Romans in A.D. 70 and their people even more scattered about than before, had good cause to find consolation in the hope that another Esther or Mordecai would rise up."[7]

The fact that some Christians in the early centuries of church history failed to accept the canonicity of the book of Esther is not crucial for at least two reasons. First, the limits of the Jewish canon were not determined through the church but through Israel (cf. Rom. 9:4). Second, during the intertestament era and the early centuries of the Christian era the true nature and purpose of the nation of Israel in the eternal plan of God became very obscure. The writing and wide acceptance of "The Greek Additions to Esther" (c. 100 B.C.), with its artificial attempt to "spiritualize" the canonical book by providing religious motives and words for Esther and Mordecai, simply demonstrates the fundamental misunderstanding of the book that characterized most Jews and Christians during those centuries.

Moore claims that Christians of the East "who lived in greater proximity to Jewish centers" generally rejected the canonicity of the book, but that Christians of the West (such as Hilary, Rufinus, and Augustine; and even, possibly, Clement of Rome, in the first century of the Christian era) tended to accept its canonicity.[8] But Moore's "Map illustrating the canonical status of Esther in the early Christian Church"[9] seems to contradict this view. The Eastern witnesses to the canon that were closest to Palestine (at Con-

7. Moore, p. xxiv.
8. Ibid., pp. xxv, xxviii.
9. Ibid., pp. xxvi-xxvii.

stanti in Cyprus, Damascus in Syria, and even Caesarea and Jerusalem in Palestine) all accepted the canonicity of Esther. The diversity of early Christian opinion on this subject, especially in the light of widespread ignorance of the true purpose of the book, really proves nothing concerning the canonicity of the book of Esther.

HISTORICITY

As our knowledge of ancient Near Eastern history increases through archaeological discovery and careful reexamination of previously available documents, the radical criticism of the book of Esther that characterized the nineteenth and early twentieth centuries becomes less and less credible. At the beginning of this century Lewis B. Paton asserted that "the Book of Esther is not historical, and it is doubtful whether even a historical kernel underlies its narrative."[10] Such a statement may now be placed into the museum of hopelessly unscientific (to say nothing of un-Christian) opinions about the book.

What is the correct basis for our approach to the historicity of Esther? The Christian frankly acknowledges his bias toward the complete historical truth of the canonical books of the Bible out of respect for the clear and repeated statements of his Lord, Jesus Christ.[11] He is willing, therefore, to take the text at face value, assuming that the author knew vastly more about the precise circumstances surrounding the events he describes than we do. Clearly recognizing, in the very nature of the case, that it is impossible to expect total extrabiblical confirmation of each biblical statement, the Christian nevertheless renders prior authority to Scripture. Extrabiblical sources are not inspired. Only Scripture is "God-

10. Paton, p. 75.
11. See "The Chicago Statement on Biblical Inerrancy," available from International Council on Biblical Inerrancy, P.O. Box 13261, Oakland, California 94661.

breathed" (2 Tim. 3:16, literal translation) and therefore completely authoritative and dependable.

It is not at all surprising, therefore, that a vast chasm separates the conservative approach to the book of Esther from the liberal approach. No writer can totally avoid theological and philosophical bias. The question is: *which* bias guides the particular investigator? Note, for example, the honest confession of Carey A. Moore: "As the reader will soon discover, Herodotus' *History of the Persian Wars* is not only a practical source for the present-day historian's knowledge of much ancient Persian history and culture *but also a major criterion by which the possible historicity and authenticity of numerous 'facts' in Esther are to be judged.*"[12] If one assumes, at the outset, that a Greek historian describing Persian court life from the perspective of an outsider is more dependable than the author of the book of Esther, then one's conclusions concerning the historicity of the book of Esther are clearly predetermined.

But what, precisely, are the major objections to the historicity of the book that Lewis Paton and Carey Moore, two of the leading negative critics of Esther in our century, have singled out? Paton's long list of objections includes three major ones.

(1) "The chief personages of the book, Vashti, Haman, Esther, Mordecai, are unknown in history."[13] But the situation is profoundly different today from what it was when Paton's book was first published (1908). J. Stafford Wright and William H. Shea[14] have shown how the name *Vashti* could be a transliteration of *Amestris,* the name Herodotus

---

12. Moore, p. xlv, italics added.
13. Paton, p. 65.
14. J. Stafford Wright, "The Historicity of Esther," in J. Barton Payne, ed., *New Perspectives on the Old Testament* (Waco, Tex.: Word, 1970), pp. 37-47, and William H. Shea, "Esther and History," *Andrews University Seminary Studies* 14, no. 1 (Spring 1976):227-46.

assigns to Xerxes' first queen (cf. my comments below on 1:9-12). *Haman* "the Agagite" (3:1) was not a descendant of the Agag whom Samuel executed, but came from a region in Media named *Agag* (cf. my comments below on 3:1). As for *Esther,* the circumstantial evidences for the existence of a second queen in Xerxes' court and harem have been set forth by William Shea in his article, "Esther and History" (cf. my comments below on 2:16-18). And last, but not least, *Mordecai* has begun to emerge from the darkness of historical obscurity (outside of Scripture) to such an extent that even Carey Moore now admits: "Mordecai may very well have been a historical personage"[15] (cf. my comments below on 2:5-6).

(2) "The statement that the laws of the Medes and Persians could not be altered (1:19, 8:8) . . . is unconfirmed by any ancient evidence."[16] J. Stafford Wright, however, convincingly demonstrates that such evidence does exist (cf. my comments below on 1:19-20).

(3) Esther could never have been Xerxes' queen, for the testimony of Herodotus 3.84 is that "the Queen might be selected only from seven of the noblest Persian families."[17] However, Wright has clearly answered this objection also (cf. my comments below on 1:14).

Two generations after Paton, Carey A. Moore seems more cautious in his accusations against the historicity of the book. After selecting a few of Paton's "improbable" statements in Esther, he cautions: "Though improbable, these things may of course still have been true."[18] But even the "more serious contradictions" in the book (listed above under Paton's objections) do not seem crucial to Moore: "Taken individually, few, if any, of these improbabilities and contradictions are

15. Moore, p. L.
16. Paton, p. 72.
17. Ibid.
18. Moore, p. xlv.

sufficiently serious to undermine the essential historicity of Esther."[19]

In addition to all of this, Moore provides various evidences in support of the book's historicity. He begins:

> On the face of it, the story seems to be true. Apart from the supposed irrevocability of Persian laws and perhaps the battle fatalities for the thirteenth of Adar in 9:16, nothing in the book seems improbable, let alone unbelievable, especially since the plot centers around court intrigue and ethnic prejudices. Moreover, the author, who begins his work in the manner typical of biblical histories, encourages his readers to confirm the details of his account for themselves by referring them to an accessible and well-known historical record (cf. 10:2). Only a writer acting in good faith would dare extend such an invitation to his readers. Then too, the book itself abounds in evidence that the author knew much about the time, place, and setting for his story. . . . Much that the author says about Xerxes seems to be quite compatible with what we know of him from other literary and archaeological sources.[20]

(See also the remarkable statements quoted from Moore in my comments on 2:16-18.)

In conclusion, the confidence that God's people through the centuries have placed in the book of Esther has been greatly confirmed during our generation. No historian could rightly demand that every detail of the book be confirmed by outside evidence. In the very nature of the case this is totally beyond the limits of scientific historiography. At the same time, it is now more obvious than ever before that no statement in the book can be proven erroneous. In view of the abundance of names, dates, places, and customs mentioned in the book, this is so remarkable that it places Esther into a vastly higher realm of reality than the apocryphal books of

19. Ibid., p. xlvi.
20. Ibid., p. xxxv.

Judith and Tobit with which it is often compared. Of the book of Esther, as of all other parts of canonical Scripture, the Christian can confidently affirm: "Thy word is truth" (John 17:17).

PURPOSE

What can be said for the religious purpose or message of a book in the Bible that mentions a certain Persian king 190 times in 167 verses but mentions God not at all? How can one properly fit into the Jewish canon a book that is full of crisis and danger to the nation but refrains from any reference to Jerusalem, the Temple, the Law, the Covenant, sacrifice, prayer, love, or forgiveness? This, of course, is the major reason the canonicity (if not the historicity) of the book has been challenged by some leading Jewish and Christian thinkers for over two thousand years. This is also probably the reason Esther has not been found among the Qumran manuscripts.

Martin Luther is recorded to have said at one time in his career: "I am so great an enemy to the second book of the Maccabees, and to Esther, that I wish they had not come to us at all, for they have too many heathen unnaturalities."[21] Most Christian scholars, of course, are less outspoken, but they nevertheless harbor much doubt and confusion as to the true message God wants to convey to His people through this portion of His holy Word.

The basic problem can be traced to a lack of discernment with regard to God's program for Israel as distinct from His program for the church. If distinctively Christian goals and ministries are superimposed on the Old Testament, or even on the four gospels, the result will inevitably be confusion and frustration. If this is true of such theocratically norma-tive accounts as Leviticus, Joshua, or even Chronicles, it is

---

21. Martin Luther, *The Table Talk of Martin Luther,* new ed., ed. and trans. William Hazlitt (London: Bohn, 1857), p. 11. [Section xxiv of *Table Talk.*]

even more true of non-normative situations described in Judges, parts of Samuel and Kings, but especially in the book of Esther.

The problem is actually twofold. In the first place, the very idea of an Israelite theocracy is offensive to many Christians today. Can we take seriously the idea that God delivered millions of Israelites from Egyptian bondage and settled them in Canaan when doing so involved the death of vast numbers of Egyptians and Canaanites? Is this not contradictory to "the Christian ethic"?

The second problem is even more serious. How could this holy God of Israel continue to destroy Gentiles, not just in Palestine, but throughout the Persian Empire in the days of King Xerxes, and then record this slaughter in the book of Esther without any reference to Himself or to any of His revealed theocratic institutions?

The answer to the first question is found in the fundamental attributes of God and the nature of post-Adamic man in the light of God's eternal purposes. Sinful men do not *deserve* to live on God's earth. This is the basic message of the Genesis Flood. God is absolutely holy; but He is also gracious, and has determined to bless nations in proportion to their response to His message through one nation, Israel, created by His sovereign grace (Gen. 12:1-3; Deut. 7:6-11). Nations and individuals that hated Israel thus demonstrated their rejection of God's gracious plan of salvation and were consigned to destruction.

It is important to note that this negative or violent aspect of the Israelite theocracy was not optional. It was not to be left to the baser or unregenerate members of the nation. Indeed, the most spiritual men (e.g., Abraham, Moses, Joshua, Samuel, David) were called upon by God to kill others for the furtherance of His purposes on earth. For Jews to have adopted the pacifistic attitude of "live and let live" toward idolatrous Gentiles in Palestine would have been to invite divine judgment (cf. Judg. 1-2).

Such a tragedy is what finally happened. Because of centuries of disobedience to the theocratic program of their God, especially in religious compromise with Gentile neighbors, first the northern tribes (722 B.C.) and then Judah (586 B.C.) were deported and scattered throughout Mesopotamia and beyond. The outward forms of the theocracy were smashed by Gentile nations that hated the God of Israel.

However, in 536 B.C., only half a century before the opening scenes of the book of Esther, fifty thousand Jews were led by their gracious God to return to Jerusalem under the leadership of a governor named Zerubbabel and a high priest named Joshua. They joyously set up an altar of sacrifice and began to rebuild their Temple. Thus Jerusalem again became the center of God's redemptive program for the entire world (Hag. 2; Zech. 4). Many godly Jews like Daniel could not return with this expedition. But their hearts were there (cf. Ps. 137:4-6; Dan. 6:10). To be sure, we find living in Babylon (Ezra 7) and in Susa (Neh. 1-2) many years later young men who loved their God. But the crucial and very obvious point is that when the opportunity came, they fulfilled the desire of their heart by returning to Jerusalem to further God's theocratic program.

The situation described in the book of Esther, however, is vastly different from that of Zerubbabel, Joshua, Ezra, and Nehemiah. And this supplies for us the key to the solution of our second major problem. There seems to be no evidence that Mordecai or Esther harbored any desire to relate to the heart of God's theocratic program by journeying to Jerusalem, offering the prescribed Mosaic sacrifices on the altar through Levitical priests, and praying to Jehovah in His holy Temple. Nor is any evidence given that they were in any way prevented from going.

Now the personal relationship of Mordecai and Esther to the God of Israel is not a mere academic question. Upon the proper answer to this question rests, to a large degree, the explanation of the absence of God's name in the book, the place of the book in the Hebrew canon, and the theocratic relationship of modern Israel to God. For these and other reasons, the question has been seriously debated through the centuries and deserves careful analysis.

That both the hero and the heroine of the book exhibited some elements of high moral character will be conceded by almost all careful students. This is particularly evident in the crisis of Esther 4 when Mordecai, in his appeal to Esther to appear before the king on behalf of her people (4:13-14), made a veiled reference to the providence of God in light of the Abrahamic Covenant and when Esther asked the Jews of Susa to "fast for me" (4:16) for three days while she prepared to go to the king at the very risk of her life.

While all of this may be granted, our Lord's analysis of the Jews of His day, who readily made such appeals to the Abrahamic Covenant (Matt. 3:9; John 8:39) and who spent much of their time in fasting (Matt. 6:16), should warn us that more positive evidences than these must be found to classify a particular Jew as belonging to the true "remnant" of Israel (Isa. 4:2-3; cf. John 1:47 and Rom. 9:6-8). There are, after all, in Israel today many "Mordecais" and "Esthers" who demonstrate great courage and nobility in their determination to die, if necessary, for the perpetuation of their nation and even of their religion. But it must also be sadly recognized that very few of these courageous Israelis know the God of their fathers in the sense of trusting in His provision of eternal salvation through the merits of the Messiah (cf. Isa. 53; Rom. 11:25, 28).

It must be acknowledged that Esther wanted to be a wife of Xerxes, who was a zealous Zoroastrian. She was not forced into the king's harem against her will (cf. my comments on 2:8). Furthermore, she concealed her nationality by eating nonkosher foods for many months (2:9). "Certainly, this casts Esther in a very bad light. Not only is her failure to observe the dietary regulations against her, but so is her disregard for the authority of the Law. She does not display the 'Judaism at any cost' spirit that distinguishes Daniel and even the apocryphal Judith. . . . She kept her secret for at least five years [cf. 2:16; 3:7]. For the masquerade to last that long, she must have done more than eat, dress and live like a Persian. She must have worshiped like one!"[22] "Despite the insistence of 2:20 that Esther concealed her identity as a Jew because Mordecai had so instructed her, the impression remains that Esther's Jewishness was more a fact of birth than of religious conviction."[23]

A similar problem faces us with regard to the spirituality of Mordecai. It is unthinkable that a godly Jew would have concealed his identity for a long period of time and have commanded another to do the same. Under the circumstances, this cannot be reconciled with the intent of the first of the Ten Commandments. Nor can his refusal to bow before Haman be explained on the basis of religious convictions (cf. my comments on 3:2 and 3:4). J. Stafford Wright concludes: "The Christian judgment of the Book of Esther has been unnecessarily cramped through our feeling that because Mordecai is a Bible character, he must be a good man. . . . Like Jehu he may have been little more than a time-server. The Bible makes no moral judgment upon him, but it expects us to use our Christian sense. He was raised up by God, but he was not necessarily a godly man."[24]

Seen in the true light of God's revealed program for the

---

22. Carl A. Baker, "An Investigation of the Spirituality of Esther" (M. Div. thesis, Grace Theol. Sem., 1977), pp. 21-22.
23. Moore, p. liv.
24. Wright, p. 45.

Israelite theocracy, the death of 75,000 Jew-hating Gentiles throughout the Persian Empire during the reign of Xerxes cannot provide a valid objection to the inspiration and canonicity of the book (cf. my comments on 8:11) any more than the death of the firstborn throughout Egypt constitutes an objection to the inspiration of the book of Exodus. These inspired books show us that God took the Abrahamic Covenant seriously. In the one case miraculously and in the other case providentially, God thwarted Satan's desperate efforts to destroy His covenant people. Apart from the Exodus, Israel's descendants would have been ultimately absorbed and paganized by idolatrous Egyptians. Thus, no Christ and no salvation for the world.

But Purim is no less significant for this reason. Many Jews have secularized the feast (as, indeed, they have effectively secularized their entire religion [cf. Isa. 1 and Matt. 23]). In fact, the *Talmud* (Megillah 7b) recommended that Jews were to drink wine at the celebration of Purim until they were unable to distinguish between "Blessed be Mordecai!" and "Cursed be Haman!" But this profanation cannot obscure the marvelous providence of God in the breathtaking suspense of this great drama of divine and satanic confrontation worked out on the stage of history, with God's hand (though not as empirically visible as at the Exodus) clearly discernible behind the curtains. It must not be forgotten that if Haman's plot had succeeded, not only Jews in Susa but also the theocratic community in Jerusalem would have been wiped out. As Jacob Hoschander observed, no Purim would have meant no Israel, which would mean no Christianity.[25]

Why, then, were God's name and all theocratic ideas obviously and meticulously avoided throughout the book? It was *not* because God's presence was vague or uncertain.

25. Jacob Hoschander, *The Book of Esther in the Light of History* (Philadelphia: Dropsie College, 1923), p. 10.

Nor was it because thousands of Gentiles died at the hands of Jews. Nor was it even because the Jewish hero and heroine of the book were probably unregenerate.

The true reason is that Mordecai, Esther, and the Jews of Susa not only were outside of the promised land but, moreover, were not even concerned about God's theocratic program centered in that land. On the other hand, God *did* identify Himself officially with unregenerate and wicked Jews who held royal or priestly positions within the theocracy—Jews like Saul, Ahaz, Zedekiah, and even such men as Ahab and Jehoram in the northern kingdom. This crucial distinction was lost upon the Jews of the intertestament period who tried to improve on the book of Esther by their apocryphal *Additions to Esther.* Through such an absurd and deliberate rejection of the warnings of Deuteronomy 4:2*a;* 12:32; and Proverbs 30:6 ("do not add to His words lest . . . you be proved a liar"), these intertestament Jews succeeded in permanently distorting the message of God through the book of Esther.

This, we believe, provides the best ultimate explanation for the omission of the name of Jehovah. To suggest that this name would offend Persian officials and therefore all references to Him were carefully excluded from the book is to take a low view of the inspiration of Scripture. A generation ago John Urquhart properly concluded that "the history of God's work in the earth can never be associated" with the unbelieving Jews who deliberately detach themselves from God's revealed program. "In His providence He will watch over and deliver them; but their names and His name will not be bound together in the record of the labor and the waiting for the earth's salvation."[26] Edward J. Young and Glea-

26. John Urquhart, "Esther, Book of," in *The International Standard Bible Encyclopaedia,* 5 vols., ed. James Orr (Grand Rapids: Eerdmans, 1946), 2:1009.

son L. Archer concur with this view.[27]

The undeniable providence of God as seen in His watching over His people in the detailed events of this amazing book, coupled with the complete omission of His name (to say nothing of the absence of supernatural interventions), point to both the tragedy and the hope of Israel today. Even though many Jews *are* back in the land of promise, Israel, as a nation, is completely unregenerate and has absolutely *no* access to the theocratic institutions of the Old Testament. Israel has both seen and rejected her Messiah. As the original, natural branches of the olive tree of God's blessing, Israel has been broken off (Rom. 11:16-22). Therefore, the Holy Spirit warns the church through the apostle to the Gentiles, "from the standpoint of the gospel they are enemies for your sake" (Rom. 11:28). This is the tragedy of Israel today.

But the book of Esther is a divine message of hope for Israel as well. Even in her unsaved condition, cut through unbelief from her God-given institutions, she has not been forgotten by her God. The nations of the world may have long since forgotten His Covenant with Abraham. But Jehovah has not. "Behold, He who keeps Israel will neither slumber nor sleep" (Ps. 121:4). It is true that He broke her from His tree of blessing. But it is also amazingly true that "they [Israel] also, if they do not continue in their unbelief, will be grafted in; for God is able to graft them in again" (Rom. 11:23). How can this be? The answer comes clearly: "I do not want you, brethren, to be uninformed of this mystery . . . that a partial hardening has happened to Israel until the fulness of the Gentiles has come in; and thus all Israel will be saved" (Rom. 11:25-26). Is Israel truly

27. Edward J. Young, *An Introduction to the Old Testament* (Grand Rapids: Eerdmans, 1949), p. 349, and Gleason L. Archer, *A Survey of Old Testament Introduction,* rev. ed. (Chicago: Moody, 1974), p. 417.

an enemy of God today, unworthy even of His official name? Yes, and tragically so (cf. 1 Thess. 2:14-16). "But from the standpoint of God's choice they are beloved for the sake of the fathers; for the gifts and the calling of God are irrevocable" (Rom. 11:28-29). This is Israel's hope and the hope of the world (Rom. 11:12-16).

And this is the mystery and the message of the book of Esther to our world today. Divine rejection and yet divine providence. Tragedy—and yet hope. Little did Mordecai realize that Purim could not solve the real tragedy. For untold millions of Jews his warning to Esther has found fulfillment: "You and your father's house will perish" (Est. 4:14). But he also spoke beyond his knowledge when he promised her: "Relief and deliverance will arise for the Jews from another place" (4:14). That other "place" proved to be none other than Israel's own Messiah, who spoke with infinitely greater authority and knowledge of Israel's tragedy and hope: "How often I wanted to gather your children together . . . and you were unwilling. Behold, your house is being left to you desolate! For I say to you, from now on you shall not see Me until you say, 'BLESSED IS HE WHO COMES IN THE NAME OF THE LORD!' " (Matt. 23:37-39).

1

VASHTI DEMOTED

(1:1-22)

ON THE LAST DAY of a seven-day feast in the royal city of Susa, King Xerxes called for Queen Vashti to appear before his drunken nobles to show her beauty. Her refusal provoked the king's wrath, and he followed the advice of Memucan, one of the chief princes, that she be demoted by a public decree in order that all wives throughout the Medo-Persian Empire might honor their husbands.

1. In the days of Ahasuerus. This can be none other than the Hebrew name of that capricious, cruel, but by no means inconsequential emperor of Persia from 486 to 465 B.C. whose true name was Khshayarsha and who was known among the Greeks as Xerxes. Although Josephus followed the Septuagint translators in their mistaken notion that this was Xerxes' son Artaxerxes, modern scholarship almost unanimously identifies him as Xerxes. For example, the liberal theologian Lewis B. Paton could say:

> With the identification of Ahasuerus with Xerxes all the statements of the Book of Esther agree. He was a Persian king who also ruled over Media (1:3, 18), his empire extended from India to Ethiopia and contained 127 satrapies (1:1, 8:9, 9:30), it also included the islands of the Mediterranean (10:1), his capital was at Susa in Elam (1:2,

etc.). *This is all true of Xerxes, but of no other Persian monarch.* The character of Ahasuerus, as portrayed in the Book of Esther, also agrees well with the account of Xerxes given by Herodotus and other Greek historians. *For these reasons there is general agreement among modern scholars, Jewish, Catholic, and Protestant, that by Ahasuerus the author of the Book of Esther means Xerxes.*[1]

An important biblical piece of evidence for the identification of Xerxes is Ezra 4:5-7, which places this Ahasuerus after Cyrus and Darius and *before* Artaxerxes.[2] Xerxes must also be the king referred to in Daniel 11:2 as the fourth and richest of the Persian kings, the one who would "arouse the whole empire against the realm of Greece."

In his great campaign against Greece from 481 to 479 B.C., with an army of probably two hundred thousand men and a navy of many hundreds of ships, Xerxes desperately sought to avenge the humiliating defeat suffered by his father, Darius I (522-486 B.C.), at the battle of Marathon (490 B.C.). But in spite of remarkably skillful planning and strategy, his army was nearly blocked by Spartans at the pass of Thermopylae and was defeated at Plataea, northwest of Athens (479 B.C.), soon after his great navy was smashed before his very eyes at Salamis, to the west of Athens (480 B.C.).[3]

1. Lewis B. Paton, *Esther,* International Critical Commentary (New York: Scribner's, 1908), p. 54, italics added. See also William H. Shea, "Esther and History," *Andrews University Seminary Studies* 14, no. 1 (Spring 1976):288, n. 4.

2. See J. Finegan, *Light from the Ancient Past,* 2nd ed. (Princeton: Princeton U., 1959), p. 238, and Robert Gordis, *Megillat Esther* (New York: Ktav, 1974), p. 5.

3. For the full story, see A. T. Olmstead, *History of the Persian Empire* (Chicago: U. of Chicago, 1948), pp. 248-61, and especially C. Hignett, *Xerxes' Invasion of Greece* (Oxford: Oxford U., 1963), and A. R. Burn, *Persia and the Greeks: The Defense of the West 546-478 B.C.* (New York: Minerva, 1968), pp. 318-546. For illustrative paintings, see National Geographic Society, *Greece and Rome* (Washington, D.C.: Nat. Geog. Soc., 1968), pp. 148-63.

It was especially in the last three volumes of his *Persian Wars* that Herodotus (485?-425? B.C.) excelled as a historian.[4] Although Herodotus did have a few positive things to say about Xerxes, he and especially later Greek historians such as Ctesias, Xenophon, Strabo, and Plutarch have painted for us the traditional portrait of Xerxes as an incompetent and corrupt ruler. But the other side of the administrative record of this Persian monarch has now begun to appear as archaeologists have made available to us inscriptions and monuments in various parts of his vast empire.

> A study of Persian records indicates that Xerxes was a far more successful ruler than Herodotus would suggest. The son of Darius and Queen Atossa, herself the daughter of Cyrus and sister of Cambyses, Xerxes was born to the purple, and for the last twelve years of his father's reign served as viceroy of Babylon. No sooner had he ascended the throne than first Egypt and then Babylon rebelled against him. He quelled both revolts quickly and exacted very harsh penalties on the offenders. . . . With this background, he was well equipped on the death of his father to take over Darius' two unfinished tasks: the conquest of Greece and the completion of the royal palace at Persepolis. As everyone knows, Xerxes failed completely in the first. . . . But as only too few general readers know, Xerxes was highly successful in his second task: the building of Persepolis.[5]

Although Xerxes was a worshiper of Ahuramazda and showed far less tolerance of other religions and their temples than did his royal predecessors, he was not a pure Zoroastrian. "In spirit Xerxes is further removed from Zoroaster than was his father, but he seems to have consciously adhered to the later and admittedly distorted form of the Prophet's

---

4. Cf. Hignett, pp. 25-40, and Burn, pp. 1-17.
5. Carey A. Moore, *Esther,* The Anchor Bible (Garden City, N.Y.: Doubleday, 1971), p. xxxviii.

religion as interpreted to him by the Magi."[6]

The Ahasuerus who reigned from India to Ethiopia. In order to avoid possible confusion with the Ahasuerus (Dan. 9:1) whose son, Darius the Mede, was governor of all former Babylonian provinces under Cyrus the Great from 539 to about 525 B.C., the author points to the vast territory over which Xerxes ruled (cf. Est. 8:9; 10:1).[7]

The "India" referred to here (Heb. *hōddû* = the Indus River in Sanskrit) is equivalent to the province of Punjab in Pakistan today. Herodotus, the great Greek historian of the fifth century B.C., tells us that both India and Ethiopia (Heb. *kûš*) were subject to Xerxes (3.94-98; 7.9), India having been conquered by his father, Darius I, and Ethiopia by Cambyses (530-522 B.C.). Even more important than this testimony is the discovery at Persepolis of a foundation tablet that reads in part: "Thus speaks king Xerxes: These are the countries—in addition to Persia—over which I am king under the 'shadow' of Ahuramazda: . . . India . . . (and) Kush."[8]

Over 127 provinces. Some scholars have considered this to be in contradiction to Herodotus, who listed only twenty satrapies for Darius I (3.89-94), and to the book of Daniel, which refers to 120 satraps appointed by Darius the Mede (Dan. 6:1). However, the word "provinces" (Heb. *mᵉdînâ*) here refers to the smaller governmental (or racial) units of the empire, such as the province of Judah (Neh. 1:3), whereas Herodotus was referring to the larger taxation units, such as the fifth satrapy, which included all of Phoenicia,

---

6. Burn, p. 316, quoting R. C. Zaehner, *The Dawn and Twilight of Zoroastrianism,* The Putnam History of Religion (New York: Putnam, 1961), p. 161. See also Robert J. Littman, "The Religious Policy of Xerxes and the Book of Esther," *The Jewish Quarterly Review,* n.s. 65, no. 3 (January 1975):145-55.

7. Cf. John C. Whitcomb, *Darius the Mede* (Nutley, N.J.: Presby. & Ref., 1963), pp. 17-24.

8. James B. Pritchard, ed., *Ancient Near Eastern Texts,* 3rd ed. (Princeton: Princeton U., 1969), p. 316. For the original text, see Roland G. Kent, *Old Persian* (New Haven: Am. Oriental Soc., 1953), p. 151.

Palestine, Syria, and Cyprus (3.91). On the other hand, the book of Daniel speaks of neither of these territorial units, for it merely states that Darius the Mede "appoint[ed] 120 satraps over the kingdom." (Dan. 6:1).[9]

2. *King Ahasurerus sat on his royal throne which was in Susa the capital.* Susa (the Greek name), or Shushan (the Hebrew name), was an ancient capital of Elam which Darius I rebuilt as the winter capital of the Persian Empire. It was unbearably hot in the summer, so a summer capital was established at Ecbatana (modern Hamadan) in the mountains two hundred miles to the north (cf. Ezra 6:1-2). Other capitals were Babylon, two hundred miles to the west, and Pasargadae and, later, Persepolis, both three hundred miles to the southeast.

It is fascinating to realize that the city of Susa, in which the events of the book of Esther occurred, was visited by Daniel in 551 B.C. in a vision (Dan. 8:1-8) in which he foresaw the rapid rise of the Medo-Persian Empire (which began a year later in the great victory of Cyrus over the aged and corrupt Astyages the Mede). Daniel also beheld the later victories of Alexander the Great over the Persian Empire (332-323 B.C.). Another interesting note is that in 446-445 B.C., a generation after the events of the book of Esther, we find Nehemiah serving in Susa as cupbearer to Artaxerxes during the winter months from December to March (cf. Neh. 1:1—2:1).[10]

3. *In the third year of his reign, he gave a banquet.* This great feast (Heb. *mišteh,* literally "a drinking feast"; this

9. Cf. Whitcomb, pp. 31-33.
10. The fascinating history of Susa and the other great imperial sites of the Persian Empire has been described by Roman Ghirshman, *The Arts of Ancient Iran* (New York: Golden, 1964), pp. 137-208, and by Charles F. Pfeiffer and Howard F. Vos, *The Wycliffe Historical Geography of Bible Lands* (Chicago: Moody, 1967), pp. 263-87. See also Edwin M. Yamauchi, "The Achaemenid Capitals," *Near East Archaeological Society Bulletin,* n.s. 8 (1976): 5-81. One scholar who denies the historicity of Esther concedes that "excavations of the site have not disproved the statements, admittedly vague, made about Susa in Esther" (Moore, p. 5).

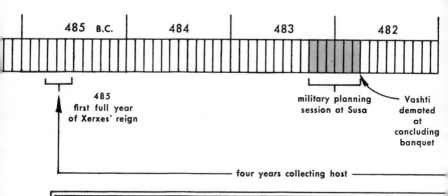

CHART OF SOME EVENTS COVERED

same Heb. word is used in Judg. 14:10 for Samson's wedding feast) and the six months of deliberations that preceded it took place in 483/482 B.C. The purpose of this great gathering is not explained, but it is almost certainly the one in which Xerxes laid plans for the invasion of Greece. Herodotus thus describes the momentous occasion:

> Xerxes, being about to take in hand the expedition against Athens, called together an assembly of the noblest Persians, to learn their opinions, and to lay before them his own designs. So, when the men were met, the king spoke thus to them: . . . My intent is to throw a bridge over the Hellespont and march an army through Europe against Greece, that thereby I may obtain vengeance from the Athenians for the wrongs committed by them against the Persians and against my father [7.8].[11]

Herodotus also explains that "reckoning from the recovery of Egypt [in the first full year of Xerxes' reign—485 B.C.],

11. All my quotations from Herodotus are from George Rawlinson's translation in Francis R. B. Godolphin, ed., *The Greek Historians,* 2 vols. (New York: Random House, 1942).

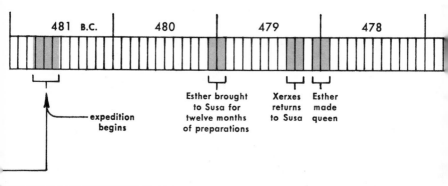

expedition begins

Esther brought to Susa for twelve months of preparations

Xerxes returns to Susa

Esther made queen

IN THE BOOK OF ESTHER

Xerxes spent four full years in collecting his host, and making ready all things that were needful for his soldiers" (7.20). The great expedition against Greece then began in the spring of 481 B.C. It is worth noting that the biblical record of and date for this six-month show of military and royal power (see my comments on Est. 1:4-5) are matched beautifully by the facts of secular history: the show of power rightly took place when the visitors were present, it took place when the troops were gathering for the expedition, and it took place before the expedition left for Greece.[12]

Liberal theologians, wholly committed to their antisupernaturalistic presuppositions, such as their belief that Scripture is not totally inspired by God and is therefore not always true in its historical content, remain unmoved by such marvelous and (to them) unexpected harmonizations between sacred and secular history. Thus we are told that "these speculations in regard to the reason for the feast are of interest

12. See Shea, p. 231.

only if one is convinced of the strictly historical character of the book."[13]

Equally significant and impossible to explain away as mere literary coincidence is the four-year interval between the demotion of Vashti in 482 B.C. (1:3) and the crowning of Esther in 479 B.C. (2:16). (See my comments on 2:1 and 2:16.) Such a chronological break in the flow of the narrative is what one might expect if, as the Greek historians inform us, Xerxes was involved at that time in his military campaign against the Greeks. Carey A. Moore insists that the biblical text "does not say why it took four years after the deposing of Vashti to find her successor" and then goes on to observe that "those who maintain the historicity of Esther often cite the fact that Xerxes would have been away in Greece for two of these four years," as if Xerxes' absence were a surprising and unwarranted explanation of the four-year gap.[14] The possibility that God's Word is indeed historically accurate and that such circumstantial evidences for its historicity are convincing proof of its accuracy has apparently escaped the modern negative critic.

The army officers of Persia and Media, the nobles, and the princes of his provinces being in his presence. In the days of Darius the Mede (a subordinate of Cyrus), two generations earlier, Media was normally mentioned before Persia (cf. Dan. 6:8), but now Persia is far more prominent in the dual monarchy. "The nobles" and "the princes" represent the civil rulers of the empire in contrast to the military leaders.

4-5. During the 180 days, Xerxes discussed war plans with his subordinates and overawed them with the opulence and grandeur of his court. After this, a seven-day feast was held (vv. 3 and 5 probably refer to the same feast[15]) *for all*

---

13. Moore, p. 12, quoting with approval Paton, p. 129.
14. Moore, p. 24.
15. See C. F. Keil, *The Books of Ezra, Nehemiah, and Esther,* trans. Sophia Taylor, Biblical Commentary on the Old Testament, by C. F. Keil and F. Delitzsch (1873; reprint ed., Grand Rapids: Eerdmans, 1950), pp. 322-24.

the people who were present in Susa the capital, including the leaders from various provinces who had come for the 180 days of planning. *The court of the garden of the king's palace.* This must refer to the grounds, or park, surrounding the palace. The entire setting confirms to the letter the prophecy of Daniel uttered in 536 B.C. that "three more kings are going to arise in Persia [Cambyses, Pseudo-Smerdis, and Darius I]. Then a fourth [Xerxes] will gain far more riches than all of them; as soon as he becomes strong through his riches, he will arouse the whole empire against the realm of Greece" (Dan. 11:2).

6. The meanings of some of these words remain obscure, but the ASV or NASB gives the general sense. White and blue (the royal colors [cf. Est. 8:15, ASV]) cotton (Heb. *karpas* = fine linen) hangings were fastened to marble pillars by means of silver rings. Also, there were gold and silver couches (cf. 7:8) on floors made of inlaid stones of various colors. This strikingly beautiful palace burned to the ground about 435 B.C., toward the end of the reign of Artaxerxes, son and successor of Xerxes.[16]

7-8. Golden vessels of various kinds. Great variety in drinking vessels was a Persian luxury. Herodotus tells us that when the Greeks defeated the Persian invaders, they found in their camp "many tents richly adorned with furniture of gold and silver, many couches covered with plates of the same, and many golden bowls, goblets, and other drinking vessels" (9.80). *According to the king's bounty.* The generosity of Solomon is similarly expressed (1 Kings 10: 13). *The drinking was done according to the law, there was no compulsion.* Usually the king pledged his guests to drink a certain amount, but now they could drink as much or as little as they desired. Herodotus reported that the Persians "are very fond of wine, and drink it in large quantities. . . . It is also their general practice to deliberate upon

16. Cf. Olmstead, p. 352.

affairs of weight when they are drunk. . . . Sometimes, however, they are sober at their first deliberation, but in this case they always reconsider the matter under the influence of wine" (1.133).

9-12. On the last day of the feast, the inebriated king sent his seven eunuchs (Heb. *sarîs;* cf. vv. 12, 15), who constituted his means of communication with the harem, to fetch Vashti. Persian queens usually ate at the king's table, but not necessarily at great banquets. Presumably fearing for her dignity in the midst of such a drunken group (cf. Herodotus 5.18), she utterly refused to obey the summons. It was under similar circumstances that a generation of Philistine nobility had been destroyed (Judges 16:25-30) and later that one of David's sons had lost his life (2 Sam. 13:28).

Critics have frequently asserted that the book of Esther is not historically accurate because Vashti is presented as the queen, whereas Herodotus identifies the queen as Amestris (9.108-13). But J. Stafford Wright has clearly shown a possible linguistic link between the Persian name Vashti and the Greek name Amestris.[17] His conclusions have been confirmed and strengthened by William H. Shea.[18] Carey A. Moore typically brushes aside the entire question: "Actually, the identity of Vashti is of crucial importance only to those modern scholars, such as Johannes Schildenberger, who have a strong apologetic interest in the *strictly* historical accurateness of Esther."[19] See my additional discussion at 2:16-18.

13. The wise men who understood the times . . . who knew law and justice. These royal advisors were thoroughly acquainted with Persian laws and customs, but even beyond that they "understood the times." This clearly implies that

---

17. J. Stafford Wright, "The Historicity of Esther," in J. Barton Payne, ed., *New Perspectives on the Old Testament* (Waco, Tex.: Word, 1970), pp. 40-42.
18. Shea, pp. 235-37.
19. Moore, p. 8.

they were astrologers and magi. See my comments on 3:7.

14. The seven princes of Persia and Media who had access to the king's presence and sat in the first place in the kingdom. It is possible that seven was a sacred number in Persia (cf. Ezra 7:14; Est. 1:10; 2:9). These names, like those of the eunuchs (v. 10), are undeniably Persian. Carey A. Moore admits that "the lack of any evidence for Greek influence in these names is certainly significant for the dating of Esther."[20]

In the year 458 B.C. (twenty-five years after Vashti's demotion), Artaxerxes decreed that Ezra be sent to Jerusalem by "the king and his seven counselors" (Ezra 7:14); this is obviously a reference to the same official body. Herodotus reported that Darius I overthrew Pseudo-Smerdis (522 B.C.) with the help of seven conspirators who were rewarded with special access to the king. Furthermore, "the king was to be bound to marry into no family excepting those of the conspirators" (Herodotus 3.84). Many scholars would concur with the opinion of Carey A. Moore that Esther, therefore, could never have become the queen of Xerxes, for "Persian queens had to come from one of the seven noble Persian families, a custom which would have automatically ruled out an insignificant Jewess."[21]

J. Stafford Wright effectively answers this objection:

> It is a pity, however, that one commentator copies another without checking the facts for himself. Certainly Darius married other wives besides one from the Seven (Herodotus III, 88); and his son, Xerxes, who succeeded him, was not the son of this wife. Xerxes' wife, Amestris, was the daughter of Otanes; but this Otanes was the son of a certain Sisamnes (Herodotus V, 25; VII, 61), while the Otanes who was one of the Seven was the son of Pharnaspes (Herodotus

20. Ibid., p. 9.
21. Ibid., p. xlvi.

III, 67). Ctesias XIII, 51, moreover, says that she was the daughter of Onophas; and he was not one of the Seven.[22]

15. According to law, what is to be done with Queen Vashti? The king was very anxious to carry out his revenge legally so that it could not be undone later.

16-18. Memucan, one of the seven princes, seized the opportunity to turn the royal family's affair into a public and national crisis, possibly because of previous conflicts between the queen and the princes. Not only would the wives of ordinary citizens defy their husbands (v. 17), but so also would the wives of the seven princes even "this day" (v. 18) demand equality through a desire to emulate their queen.

The queen's conduct will become known to all the women. . . . The ladies of Persia and Media who have heard of the queen's conduct. This is a fascinating testimony to the strict social stratification that was maintained in ancient Persia. Robert Gordis points out that "in vs. 17, the generic term *kol hannāšîm* occurs; in vs. 18, the specific term *śārôṯ pāras ûmāḏay.* Hence, the former term means 'all the women (except the ladies of the court),' i.e., the generality of women, while the latter phrase means 'the ladies of the aristocracy.' . . . This structure is not merely literary. Vashti's defiance of the king had taken place during the second feast 'for all the people' (v. 5). Their wives (v. 17) would, therefore, be the first to know of it; the women of the nobility would learn of it a little later (v. 18)."[23]

19-20. Let it be written in the laws of Persia and Media so that it cannot be repealed. This appeal to the immutability of Persian laws was apparently to protect the princes from Vashti's revenge should she ever return to power. For similar statements of the unalterability of these laws, compare Esther 8:8 and Daniel 6:8, 12, 15. Carey A. Moore is

22. Wright, pp. 38-39.
23. Robert Gordis, "Studies in the Esther Narrative," *Journal of Biblical Literature* 95, no. 1 (March 1976):46.

among the many negative critics who insist that "there is no evidence for this irrevocability of the Persian law. . . . Certainly such a law seems inflexible and crippling to good government, and, hence, improbable."[24] Even a conservative scholar like J. G. Baldwin can state that "no extrabiblical reference to the irrevocability of the laws of the Medes and Persians has come to light," though she does go on to state that in spite of this "such a doctrine is in keeping with their pride, which would be injured by an admission that their laws could be improved."[25]

It seems surprising, in light of this, that Old Testament scholars have not given more attention to the incident recorded by Diodorus Siculus (17.30) concerning Darius III (335-331 B.C.), who, in a great rage, condemned a certain Charidemus to death. Later, however, "when the King's anger abated, he at once repented and blamed himself for having made the greatest mistake, but . . . it was not possible for what was done by the royal authority to be undone."[26] (Greek: *"all' ou gar ēn dunaton to gegonos dia tēs basilikēs exousias agenēton kataskeuasai"*).[27] If this means merely that Charidemus could not be brought back from the dead, it would be, in the words of J. Stafford Wright, "a piece of sententious moralizing and would not be improved by adding 'by the royal authority.'"[28] Furthermore, "the use here of the perfect participle (*to gegonos*) and the adjective (*basilikēs*) makes the statement a general comment on Persian law"[29] instead of a mere personal experience of Darius III, especially when "the law of the Persians" is referred to about ten lines earlier. Thus, we have in a pre-Christian historian a

---

24. Moore, p. 11.
25. J. G. Baldwin, "Esther," in Donald Guthrie and Alec Motyer, eds., *The New Bible Commentary: Revised* (Grand Rapids: Eerdmans, 1970), p. 415.
26. Wright, pp. 39, 40.
27. Ibid., p. 39.
28. Ibid., p. 40.
29. Ibid.

rather clear testimony to the existence of the kind of Medo-Persian law referred to in Daniel and Esther.

Moore suggests that the omission of the title "Queen" in verse 19 (in contrast to previous verses) is probably intentional.[30]

22. He sent letters to all the king's provinces, to each province according to its script and to every people according to their language. This statement, together with similar comments on the Persian postal system in 3:13 and 8:10, 14, constitutes a major testimony to the historicity of the book of Esther. The ancient historian Herodotus of Halicarnassus (c. 484-425 B.C.), who himself traveled through the western extent of the Persian Empire not long after the reign of Xerxes, thus describes its marvelous communications system:

> Nothing mortal travels so fast as these Persian messengers. The entire plan is a Persian invention; and this is the method of it. Along the whole line of road there are men (they say) stationed with horses, in number equal to the number of days which the journey takes, allowing a man and horse to each day; and these men will not be hindered from accomplishing at their best speed the distance which they have to go, either by snow or rain, or heat, or by the darkness of night. The first rider delivers his dispatch to the second, and the second passes it to the third; and so it is borne from hand to hand along the whole line, like the light in the torch-race, which the Greeks celebrate to Hephaestus. The Persians give the riding post in this manner, the name of *angareion* [8.98].

Richard T. Hallock believes that "there may have been a change of horses at each supply station, that is, every twenty miles or so. The famed pony express (1860-61), running between St. Joseph, Missouri, and Sacramento, California,

30. Moore, p. 11.

and covering 1,838 miles in a minimum of ten days, maintained posts seven to twenty miles apart."[31]

Interesting archaeological light has been shed on this system: "In the drier and more favorable climate of Egypt there has been found a leather sack, evidently a relic of the former Persian post, containing several officially sealed parchment documents written by high Persian officials in the script and language of the Egyptian Aramaic papyri."[32]

But in spite of this ancient "pony express system," communication was greatly complicated by the scores of languages spoken throughout the empire.[33]

That every man should be the master in his own house and the one who speaks in the language of his own people. The meaning is somewhat obscure, but presumably it means that "the rule of the husband in the house was to be shown by the fact that only the native tongue of the head of the house was to be used in the family."[34] Compare the situation in Judea a generation later, where the Ashdodite wives determined the language to be spoken in some Judean homes (Neh. 13: 23-24). The decree may seem strange, especially because men normally dominated the home in the ancient Near East, but both biblical and extrabiblical evidences concur on the absurdity of various proclamations Xerxes issued. That the decree was essentially unenforceable apparently did not occur to this monarch. It must also be kept in mind that some background information about Vashti's defiance of her husband may well have been included in the final form of the decree.

31. Richard T. Hallock, *Persepolis Fortification Tablets* (Chicago: U. of Chicago, 1969), p. 6, quoted by Shea, p. 238.
32. R. A. Bowman, "Arameans, Aramaic, and the Bible," *Journal of Near Eastern Studies* 7, no. 2 (April 1948):65-90.
33. Photographs of royal decrees by Xerxes in Persian, Elamite, and Babylonian may be seen in Benjamin Mazar, ed., *Illustrated World of the Bible Library* (New York: McGraw Hill, 1961).
34. Keil, p. 332.

2

ESTHER BECOMES QUEEN

(2:1-23)

WHEN XERXES longed for Vashti again, it was proposed that a new queen be chosen for him from among the most beautiful in the land. Esther, a young Jewess who had been raised by her older cousin Mordecai, was among those brought to the royal house of the women. Xerxes loved her more than any other, and chose her to be his queen. Soon afterward, Mordecai discovered a plot against the king; through Esther the matter was reported to the king, and the criminals were executed.

1. After these things . . . he remembered Vashti. The "remembered" in this context carries the thought of affectionate remembrance. Esther became queen in December 479 or January 478 B.C. (2:16), and more than a year must have elapsed between the decree of 2:3 and her marriage (cf. 2:12), so the king's desire for Vashti must have become known while he was still engaged in his great campaign against Greece (481-479 B.C.). See my comments on 1:3 and 2:16.

2-4. Realizing that the restoration of Vashti would spell doom for them (see my note on 1:19), the courtiers (not the princes, but Xerxes' personal attendants) suggested a very bold proposition. Instead of taking a wife from among the families of the seven counselors (see my note on 1:14), he should choose a new queen from among the most beautiful virgins in the entire empire. "Little imagination is needed to appreciate the horror caused by the round-up of these girls, whose fate it was to be carried away from their homes to be secluded for life as the king's concubines. What a liability to be beautiful!"[1]

To the harem, into the custody of Hegai, the king's eunuch, who was in charge of the women. Compare verses 8 and 15. Only eunuchs had access to "the house of the women" (v. 3, KJV). *"Let the young lady who pleases the king be queen in place of Vashti." And the matter pleased the king, and he did accordingly.* "The Hebrew idiom 'be good in the eyes of' [translated 'pleases' and 'pleased' in the NASB] appears twice in this verse and must certainly be translated differently in each case. In this case (4b) the proposal seemed 'sound' rather than 'pleasant.' The king recognized the sensible political advice behind this suggestion: every king must have a queen. That his harem would be enlarged and rejuvenated was a very pleasant, but incidental, by-product of a political and social necessity."[2]

5-6. Now there was a Jew in Susa the capital whose name was Mordecai, the son of Jair, the son of Shimei, the son of Kish, a Benjaminite, who had been taken into exile from Jerusalem with the captives who had been exiled with Jeconiah king of Judah, whom Nebuchadnezzar the king of Babylon had exiled. Carey A. Moore speaks for the school of negative criticism by referring the first "who" back to Mordecai instead of to Kish and insisting that the verse is therefore unhistorical.[3] Obviously, Mordecai could not have been exiled from Jerusalem with King Jeconiah (or, Jehoia-

1. J. G. Baldwin, "Esther," in Donald Guthrie and Alec Motyer, eds., *The New Bible Commentary: Revised* (Grand Rapids: Eerdmans, 1970), p. 415.
2. Carey A. Moore, *Esther,* The Anchor Bible (Garden City, N.Y.: Doubleday, 1971), pp. 18-19.
3. Ibid., pp. 20, 26-27.

chin) in 597 B.C. and then be promoted to prime minister
of the Persian Empire 123 years later in 474 B.C.! Those
who hold to the historicity of the book will find small consolation in Moore's assurance that this genealogy "argues
somewhat for the historicity of Mordecai" because "had he
been a totally fictitious character, the author of Esther could
easily have made him a direct descendant of Saul [instead
of Kish, the father of Saul], thus setting up a perfect parallel
with Haman, who was a descendant of Agag."[4] Some conservative writers also reveal much confusion at this point.[5]
The problem has been satisfactorily solved by J. Stafford
Wright, who concludes: "If the relative pronoun applies to
the last name in the genealogy (as in 2 Chron. 22:9 and
Ezra 2:61), it was Kish, Mordecai's great-grandfather, who
was taken with Jehoiachin. In Esther 2:5-6, there are three
relative pronouns, and each refers to the name that immediately precedes."[6]

Mordecai (as well as his cousin Esther) was thus a direct
descendant of one of the ten thousand leading citizens of
Jerusalem, including Ezekiel, whom Jeremiah described as
"good figs" (Jer. 24:5) in contrast to the "bad figs" who
were left in Jerusalem with King Zedekiah. How Mordecai
or his immediate ancestors arrived in the capital city of Susa,
two hundred miles east of Babylon, we can only speculate.
As far back as 722 B.C., Sargon of Assyria had deported
tens of thousands of Israelites from Samaria to "the cities of
the Medes" (2 Kings 17:6). Possibly some of these northern
Israelites were also numbered among the Jews who lived in
Susa in the days of Mordecai and Esther.

4. Ibid., p. 19.
5. E.g., Baldwin, pp. 415-16, and C. F. Keil, *The Books of Ezra, Nehemiah, and Esther,* trans. Sophia Taylor, Biblical Commentary on the Old Testament, by C. F. Keil and F. Delitzsch (1873; reprint ed., Grand Rapids: Eerdmans, 1950), p. 336.
6. J. Stafford Wright, "The Historicity of Esther," in J. Barton Payne, ed., *New Perspectives on the Old Testament* (Waco, Tex.: Word, 1970), p. 38; cf. Gleason L. Archer, *A Survey of Old Testament Introduction,* rev. ed. (Chicago: Moody, 1974), p. 419.

In a significant article entitled "Mordecai, a Historical Problem," Siegfried H. Horn has observed that while Mordecai's name appears fifty-eight times in the ten chapters of Esther, neither he nor Haman is mentioned in any other ancient documents as prime ministers of Xerxes.[7] Liberal theologians have therefore felt at liberty to dismiss Mordecai as a fictitious character.

Even apart from the powerful endorsement of the entire Jewish canon by the Lord Jesus Christ (cf. Matt. 5:18; Luke 24:27, 44; John 10:35), the mention of Mordecai's name in connection with the Feast of Purim in the intertestamental book of 2 Maccabees (15:36) and the confirmation of the universal Jewish observance of this feast by Josephus (*Antiquities* 11.6.13) should have given great caution to those who would deny the historicity of Mordecai. For further discussion of these external testimonies to the Feast of Purim, see my discussion at 9:26. It was not uncommon for Jews of Mordecai's times to carry Babylonian names. Thus, the fact that "Mordecai" derives from the Babylonian god *Marduk* is no more problematic than for Sheshbazzar (Ezra 1:8, 11; 5:14, 16) to be named after *Shamash* the Babylonian sun god. See also my comments at 2:7 concerning Hadassah/Esther.[8] Ezra (2:2) and Nehemiah (7:7) mention another Mordecai as participating in the first return to Jerusalem. Like the apostle Paul, Mordecai was a Benjaminite but was known as a Jew (Est. 2:5; cf. Rom. 11:1; Gal. 2:15).

But now, in God's providence, new evidence for the historicity of Mordecai has come to light. Professor A. Ungnad of Berlin published in 1941 an article in which he pointed out the definite possibility that a certain *Markukâ* mentioned in a cuneiform tablet (Amherst Tablet #258) as a high

---

7. Siegfried H. Horn, "Mordecai, a Historical Problem," *Biblical Research* 9 (1964):14-25.

8. For other examples, see Horn, pp. 16-17, esp. n. 13.

official at the court of Susa during the early years of Xerxes (or late years of Darius I) could be the Mordecai of the book of Esther.[9]

The Mardukâ of this tablet appears as the trusted accountant of the well-known satrap Uštannu of Babylonia and the Region Beyond the River. "Ungnad emphasized already in his early articles on this question that 'it is improbable that there existed two Mardukâs in Susa as high officials' at that time, for which reason he 'considered it very probable, that we have in this text . . . the only extra-Biblical mentioning of Mordecai.' "[10]

In the face of such epigraphic evidence, Carey A. Moore can now permit himself "to conclude that the story of Mordecai may very well have to it a kernel of truth."[11] But this attitude of extreme skepticism seems to be the exception among scholars today. Robert Gordis, for example, believes that the discovery of the name *Mardukâ* constitutes "the strongest support thus far for the historical character of the book" and that "this identification would support the view advanced on internal grounds in this study that Mordecai held a government position after Esther's accession to the throne."[12]

7. *And he was bringing up Hadassah, that is Esther, his uncle's daughter, for she had neither father nor mother.* We learn from verse 15 that Esther's father's name was Abihail (the uncle of Mordecai). Assuming, then, that Kish was a young man when he was deported to Babylon in 597 B.C., his son Shimei could have been born about 580 B.C. Shimei's older son Jair could have been born about 550 B.C. and his

9. Arthur Ungnad, "Keilinschriftliche Beiträge zum Buch Ezra und Esther," *Zeitschrift für die alttestamentliche Wissenschaft* 58 (1940-41):240-44 and 59 (1942-43):219. Horn, p. 20; cf. Moore, p. 1, and Wright, p. 44.

10. Horn, p. 22.

11. Carey A. Moore, "Archaeology and the Book of Esther," *The Biblical Archaeologist* 38, nos. 3-4 (1975):74.

12. Robert Gordis, *Megillat Esther* (New York: Ktav, 1974), p. 6.

younger son Abihail about 545 B.C. Mordecai could have been begotten of Jair about 520 B.C. and Abihail's daughter Esther about 505 B.C., making Mordecai about fifteen years older than his cousin and making Esther about twenty-six when she became queen, in 479 or 478 B.C.

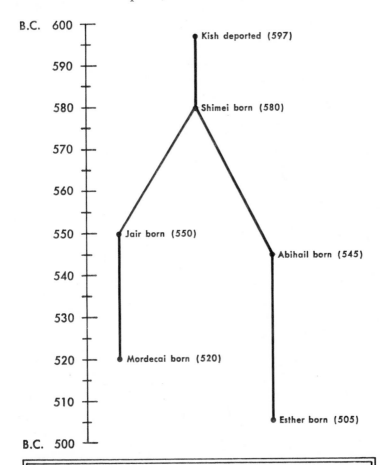

GENEALOGY FROM KISH TO ESTHER

When Daniel and his three friends were taken to Babylon, they were given official Babylonian names (Dan. 1:7). Likewise, "Esther had two names, one Hebraic and one non-Hebraic, the latter being derived from either the Persian *stâra,* 'star,' or Ishtar, the Babylonian goddess of Love."[13] As for her Hebraic name, Hadassah, "most scholars follow the Targums which interpret it to mean 'myrtle' (see Isa. 41:19, 55:13; Zech. 1:8, 10, 11): 'because' says II Targum, 'as the myrtle spreads fragrance in the world, so did she spread good works.' "[14] See also the analysis of Mordecai's name at 2:5-6.

8-9. Many young ladies were gathered to Susa the capital . . . to the king's palace. "No number is given, but there could have been many; for example, Josephus says four hundred virgins were brought. According to Plutarch, the Persian king Artaxerxes had 'three hundred and sixty concubines, all women of the highest beauty' (*Artaxerxes* XXVII.5)."[15]

The terms "capital" and "palace" constitute a parallelism, and thus "palace" here has a broader meaning than the "palace" of verse 13, where the king's actual apartments are meant. Esther's personal feelings in this matter are not recorded, but there is no biblical evidence that she abhorred the thought of becoming a concubine or queen of the pagan and corrupt Xerxes. Centuries later, perhaps about 100 B.C., a Jewish writer attempted to paint Esther as a highly spiritual woman by putting this prayer into her mouth: "You know everything; and you know that I hate the pomp of the wicked, and I loathe the bed of the uncircumcised—and of any foreigner."[16] This simply demonstrates that the true pur-

13. Moore, *Esther,* p. 20. Cf. A. S. Yahuda, "The Meaning of the Name Esther," *Journal of the Royal Asiatic Society,* 1946, pp. 174-78.
14. Moore, *Esther,* p. 20.
15. Ibid., p. 21.
16. Ibid., p. 107.

pose of the book of Esther was misunderstood already during the intertestament period. Some would find in the expression "Esther was *taken* to the king's palace into the custody of Hegai" (v. 8, italics added) the idea that this was against her will. But the verb used here (*lqḥ*) does not "suggest anything unpleasant, since it was also used by the author in verse 15 to describe Mordecai's adoption of Esther."[17]

He quickly provided her with her cosmetics and food. Because Esther did not identify her nationality (cf. v. 10), she could not have refused the ceremonially unclean food as Daniel did. The implications of this for Esther's relationship to the God of Israel and the theocratic community are quite significant. See the Introduction.

10-11. Esther did not make known her people or her kindred, for Mordecai had instructed her that she should not make them known. Why Mordecai charged her to keep her nationality secret (cf. v. 20) is not easy to determine. Possibly he feared for her safety (v. 11), or perhaps he was deeply concerned for the remnant of Israel scattered throughout the empire in the light of certain ominous developments he saw on the political horizon and hoped that somehow Esther might play an important part in delivering her people in the inevitable hour of crisis (cf. 4:14).

12-15. Six months with spices and the cosmetics for women. Carey A. Moore has recently conceded that the

> interpretation of archaeological data continues to clarify "details of fact." By proving, for instance, that certain "incense" burners found in Hureida in Hadramaut and at Lachish and Gezer in Israel were actually secular cosmetic burners, W. F. Albright showed that Hebrew *bbsmym* in Esther 2:12 really means "with cosmetic burner," not "with perfumes." Thus, we should now translate Esther 2:12b as "(for this was the prescribed length for their treatment:

17. Ibid., p. 21.

six months with oil of myrrh, and six months fumigation with other cosmetics for women)." Like the semi-nomadic Arab women of the eastern Sudan in the last century, women like Esther long, long ago fumigated themselves, saturating their hair, skin, and pores with fumes from cosmetic burners.

One thing is indisputably clear: the more one learns about the setting and general background for the story of Esther, the more fascinating and exciting the story itself becomes. In so many, many ways Esther's world was different from ours.[18]

These are rather remarkable words from a scholar who denies "the essential historicity of the Esther story."[19]

After an entire year of such preparations, the turn of each maiden came to go in to the king. For this visit she could have (or temporarily use?) any ornaments, jewelry, or apparel that she wanted. "Though these girls had every luxury, and could choose any adornment to enhance their beauty, they returned from the king's presence to the house of the concubines, mere chattels, awaiting the king's pleasure, if indeed he ever remembered them again. It is understandable that Mordecai should have wanted to make life as bearable as possible for his adopted daughter."[20]

But Esther *did not request anything except what Hegai . . . advised.* Common sense led Hegai, the eunuch in charge of of the virgins, and Esther, to avoid the excessive ornamentation that might have been appropriate for less beautiful women. It was the natural qualities of character and physical beauty that she inherited from her Jewish ancestors, not necessarily "the hidden person of the heart, with the imper-

---

18. Moore, "Archaeology and the Book of Esther," p. 78, italics added. Cf. Elizabeth Achtemeier et al., *A Light unto My Path: Old Testament Studies in Honor of Jacob M. Myers,* ed. Howard N. Bream et al., Gettysburg Theological Studies, no. 4 (Philadelphia: Temple U., 1974), pp. 25-32.
19. Moore, "Archaeology and the Book of Esther," pp. 78-79.
20. Baldwin, p. 416.

ishable quality of a gentle and quiet spirit, which is precious in the sight of God" (1 Pet. 3:4), that caused her, under God's amazing providence, to find *favor in the eyes of all who saw her* (Est. 2:15) and even to find *favor and kindness with* the mighty Xerxes (v. 17).

16-18. So Esther was taken to King Ahasuerus to his royal palace in the tenth month which is the month Tebeth, in the seventh year of his reign. This was the month of December 479 or January 478 B.C. A century ago, C. F. Keil called attention to the long delay of four years from the repudiation of Vashti in Xerxes' third year (483 B.C.), "an interval whose length cannot be adequately accounted for by the statements of the present book."[21] Esther could very easily have been made queen within two years; but the four-year interval is exactly what would be needed for Xerxes to have hurled one of the greatest armies of the ancient world against the Greeks and to suffer crushing defeats on the land and on the sea. See my further comments at 1:3 and 2:1. For the question of Xerxes' taking as his queen a woman who did not come from one of the seven noble Persian families, see my discussion at 1:14.

Perhaps one of the most popular arguments against the historical truth of the book of Esther in the thinking of scholars today is the fact that Queen Esther does not appear in any other ancient historical records. Carey A. Moore, for example, is quite dogmatic on this point: "The answer is clear; not only is there no evidence for her actual existence, but there is strong evidence against it; the queen of Xerxes then was Amestris (so Herodotus, III, 84)."[22]

Totally apart from the divine authority of Christ and His apostles concerning the absolute truth of canonical writings (see my comments on 2:5 concerning the identification of

21. Keil, p. 339.
22. Moore, "Archaeology and the Book of Esther," p. 73.

Mordecai), the amazing accuracy of the book of Esther in its depiction of life and customs in the court of Xerxes should earn for the book some measure of respect for its statements even if they cannot as yet be fully confirmed at every point by archaeological evidence.

Professor Moore himself is aware of the positive evidences for the truthfulness of the book. He states:

> The author of Esther says much which is consistent with what we know about Xerxes from non-biblical sources. For example, Xerxes' empire did extend from India to Ethiopia, . . . and Xerxes did have a winter palace at Susa (1:2), which had features not incompatible with the architectural details given in 1:5-6. Famous for his lavish drinking parties (1:4-7) and his extravagant promises and gifts (5:3, 6:6-7), Xerxes also had, on occasion, a nasty, irrational temper (1:12, 7:7-8).
>
> Moreover, the author of Esther shows awareness of certain features of Persian government, such as the seven princely advisers (1:14) and the very efficient postal system (3:13, 8:10); he is also familiar with certain practices of Persian court life, including doing obeisance to the king's high officials (3:2) and the recording and rewarding of the king's "benefactors" (2:23, 6:8). The author is also aware of various details and Persian customs, among them hanging as a form of capital punishment (2:23, 5:14, 7:10); the observance of "lucky" days (3:7); royal horses with crowns (6:8); eating while reclined on couches (7:8); and the headpiece known as a "turban" (8:15). And finally, the author uses a number of Persian nouns, including the following: *part^{e}mîm*, "nobles," 1:3; *bîtān*, "pavilion," 1:5; *karpas*, "cotton," 1:6; *dāt*, "law," 1:8; *keter*, "turban," 1:11; *pitgām*, "decree," 1:20; *'^{a}haśdarp^{e}nîm*, "satrapies," 3:12; *g^{e}nāzîm*, "treasury," 3:9; *patšegen*, "copy," 3:14; *'^{a}hašt^{e}rānîm*, "royal horses," 8:10. . . .

But taken together the arguments outlined above provide,

at best, only evidence for the author's familiarity with Persian history, customs, and vocabulary; they do not establish the essential historicity of his entire story, especially since there is some evidence to the contrary.[23]

Conservative scholars will express appreciation to Professor Moore for his careful analysis of the details of the book of Esther. But at the same time they will stand amazed at his willingness to allow a few apparently unsolved problems in the book to lower it to the level of "certain legendary stories of the ancient Near East, such as *A Thousand and One Nights.*"[24]

But such radical depreciation of the book of Esther because of extrabiblical silence on Esther herself and some testimony to the existence of a different queen (Amestris in Herodotus) invites comparison to the attitude of critics of the book of Daniel shortly before the discovery in cuneiform tablets of the existence of Belshazzar as the final de facto king of Babylon.[25] Would an author who knew so much about the court of Susa in the days of Xerxes have deliberately conjured up a nonexistent queen as one of the key persons in his history? Would the Jewish community throughout the Medo-Persian Empire have accepted as canonical a book that was tainted with such colossal historical blunders when they labeled as apocryphal such works as 1 Maccabees, Tobit, and Judith? Did not the Jewish leaders of that day have at least as much knowledge of their Persian overlords as did the Gentiles of that same time? Dr. Robert Dick Wilson, renowned for his knowledge of ancient Near Eastern history and languages, once stated: "In the name of scholarship and for the sake of truth and righteousness, it is time to call a

23. Moore, *Esther,* p. xli.
24. Ibid., p. xlvi.
25. Cf., e.g., John C. Whitcomb, *Darius the Mede* (Nutley, N.J.: Presby. & Ref., 1963), pp. 59-63.

halt on all those who presume to a knowledge which they do not possess, in order to cast reproach upon an ancient writer, as to whose sources of information and knowledge of the facts they must be ignorant and whose statements they cannot possibly fully understand, nor successfully contradict."[26]

But beyond all of these basic considerations, J. Stafford Wright and William H. Shea[27] have more carefully scrutinized the text of the book of Esther and the texts of Herodotus (*Persian Wars*) and other ancient records and have found highly convincing circumstantial evidence for the demotion of Vashti (= Amestris, cf. my comments on 1:9) and the promotion of another woman to her position as queen, at least during the years 483-473 B.C., when the events of our book occurred.

On the basis of statements by Ctesias, an ancient Greek historian (13.51, 55), Wright concludes that "Artaxerxes was eighteen when he came to the throne in 465, so he must have been born about 483; and Amestris/Vashti's refusal to appear in Esther [1:12] may well have been because she was pregnant." Furthermore, "no children were born to Amestris/Vashti after the time when the Bible says that Esther became queen."[28]

William H. Shea has also contributed a fascinating harmonization of events recorded by Herodotus and events recorded in the Bible concerning Vashti and Esther. "While at his winter quarters in Sardis [in 480/479 B.C., following the defeat of his military forces in Greece], Xerxes turned his attention from making war to making love. Herodotus reports that while he was there he fell in love with the wife of his brother Masistes, and endeavored, unsuccessfully, to

26. Robert Dick Wilson, *Studies in the Book of Daniel: A Study of the Historical Questions* (New York: Knickerbocker, 1917), p. 149.
27. William H. Shea, "Esther and History," *Andrews University Seminary Studies* 14, no. 1 (Spring 1976):227-46
28. Wright, p. 43.

carry on an affair with her (IX, 109)." In view of the fact that Herodotus does *not* mention Amestris (=Vashti) in this episode but *does* refer to her in connection with later events in Susa, it seems probable that she "was left home from this campaign whereas the wives of lesser figures were included in the royal entourage."[29] Her demotion as recorded in Esther 1 may well have been the reason for this. Furthermore, "considering Amestris' violent reaction to Xerxes' philandering upon his return to Susa, the absence of such a reaction on her part is significant since Xerxes provided just as much provocation at Sardis."[30]

"The amorous affairs of Xerxes which Herodotus describes may have been more than simply such affairs, if he was also in search of a new chief wife or queen at that time. His attention to these women under such circumstances could also explain why Amestris' reaction was so violent towards them. Position rather than affection may have been more the issue as far as Amestris was concerned, since the royal harem probably was not otherwise lacking."[31]

Professor Shea demonstrates that "the variable factors involved in the chronological references in [Herodotus] allow sufficient time for his edict to have reached Susa before Esther commenced her period of preparation, especially considering the speed with which the Persian courier service is credited."[32] Also, "it is evident that Xerxes had at least three months to return to Susa before Esther went in to him sometime in the tenth month of that seventh year [Dec. 479 or Jan. 478 B.C.]"[33]

Late in the fall of 479 B.C., now back in Susa, Xerxes again

29. Shea, p. 236.
30. Ibid., p. 235.
31. Ibid., p. 238.
32. Ibid.
33. Ibid., p. 239.

became enmeshed in an amorous affair, this time with Masistes' *daughter* Artaynte instead of Masistes' *wife*. According to Herodotus, Xerxes was more successful in romancing with this young lady (who had become his daughter-in-law in the meantime) than he was with her mother (Herodotus IX, 108-11). The matter came to a head, however, when he promised Artaynte the desire of her heart. She chose Xerxes' coat-of-many-colors, which Amestris had woven with her own hands for him (a very unqueenly activity—to ingratiate herself with him again?). Xerxes reluctantly gave her the robe, but Amestris got revenge when the time came to celebrate the king's birthday. On that occasion she asked Xerxes, Salome-like, to give her Masistes' wife, and according to the custom of the day he was obliged to comply with her request. Amestris promptly had her mutilated. As a consequence, Masistes attempted to flee to Bactria to raise a revolt against Xerxes, but the king's men caught and killed him before he reached his intended destination.[34]

Professor Shea points out that Esther 1:19 ("that Vashti should come no more into the presence of King Ahasuerus") does not mean that the king would never see her again. "As an idiom, it could be paraphrased to mean that she could not appear with Xerxes in her official capacity again [cf. 1:14]." Nevertheless, even after Xerxes returned to Susa in 479 B.C., Vashti/Amestris still had not regained her lost position of honor as queen, for "if Amestris still was Xerxes' queen at this time, why did she have to bide her time until his birthday in order to take that opportunity to get revenge upon Masistes' family [Herodotus 9.110-111]? If she still occupied her former position, would it have been necessary for her to come to the king as a suppliant on a state occasion for such a purpose?"[35]

34. Ibid., p. 240.
35. Ibid., p. 241.

"The evidence is indirect, but her absence from the winter court at Sardis, her attempt to ingratiate herself with Xerxes again by way of the coat-of-many-colors, her relative position in this affair, and her violent jealousy of other women of the royal household, all point in the direction of the idea that her status had been affected in some way or another, and the events of Esther 1 may provide an explanation for that alteration."[36]

Herodotus drops his history of Xerxes at the point of his return to Susa following the Greek campaign. "Thus it is an overstatement of the case to say that Amestris was Xerxes' queen between his 7th and 12th years, since we have no further information about her until the time her son Artaxerxes I occupied the Persian throne. . . . This silence at least allows a place in Persian history for Esther, although it does not prove that she occupied it."[37] The careful investigations of scholars such as J. Stafford Wright and William H. Shea have thus demonstrated the distinct possibility that the Vashti of the book of Esther was the Amestris of Herodotus and that this beautiful but cruel queen lost her position of high prestige during the third year of Xerxes and did not regain it even after his return to Susa in his seventh year. This constitutes a major contribution to our appreciation for the full historicity of the book of Esther.

He also made a holiday for the provinces. The Hebrew word translated "holiday" (*hᵃnāḥâ*) means, literally, "a causing to rest" and could refer to a remission of taxes or a release from military service or both. "Perhaps it is relevant that when the False Smerdis ascended the throne [522 B.C.], he granted his subjects freedom from taxation *and* military service for a period of three years (Herodotus III, 67)."[38]

36. Ibid., p. 242.
37. Ibid., p. 240-41. Cf. Moore, *Esther,* p. xlvi. Cf. also A. T. Olmstead, *History of the Persian Empire* (Chicago: U. of Chicago, 1948), pp. 308, 312, where some of the cruelties of "savage Queen-Mother Amestris" during the reign of Artaxerxes I are described.
38. Moore, *Esther,* p. 25.

19. And when the virgins were gathered together the second time. The purpose of this second gathering is not explained, but it must be remembered that Xerxes, like Solomon, was a polygamist and was constantly adding to his harem. Moore, however, appeals to Dead Sea Scroll parallels for the reading "various" instead of "the second time," thus giving the idea of "various virgins."[39] Robert Gordis suggests that "the verse refers to a second procession of the unsuccessful contestants, whose undeniable charms served to set off in more striking relief Esther's beauty. This assembling of the virgins before they were sent home took place at the conclusion of the ceremonies elevating the new queen to the throne."[40]

Mordecai was sitting at the king's gate. Throughout the ancient Near East, "the gate" was a large and elaborate structure where legal matters were settled. Herodotus, for example, spoke of two officials who sat "in the gate of the king's palace" (3.120).[41] This suggests that Mordecai had just been appointed through Esther's influence to be a magistrate or a judge, for "the king's gate" was apparently the customary meeting place for Persian officials. "It now becomes clear that 2:20 is no mere repetition or doublet of 2:10. Though Esther has been instrumental in having Mordecai named to a governmental post and he is known as a Jew, she continues to keep her Jewish origin a secret, as Mordecai has instructed her. Obviously, her role in his appointment did not *ipso facto* indicate that the queen herself was Jewish. Mordecai's official position is also directly relevant to the as-

39. Ibid., p. 30.
40. Robert Gordis, "Studies in the Esther Narrative," *Journal of Biblical Literature* 95, no. 1 (March 1976):47.
41. See figure 203 in Roman Ghirshman, *The Arts of Ancient Iran* (New York: Golden, 1964), reprinted in *Biblical Archaeologist* 38, nos. 3-4 (1975):75. See also S. Barabas, "Gate," in Merrill C. Tenney, ed., *The Zondervan Pictorial Encyclopedia of the Bible,* 5 vols. (Grand Rapids: Zondervan, 1975), 2:655-57.

sassination plot, for it facilitates his overhearing the conspiracy of the courtiers Bigthan and Teresh (v. 21)."[42]

20. Esther had not yet made known her kindred or her people. See my comments on verses 10-11 and the Introduction.

21-23. Bigthan and Teresh . . . guarded the door. These otherwise unknown officials probably "guarded the king's private apartments (Herodotus III. 77, 118)."[43] It has been speculated that these men were seeking revenge for the deposition of Vashti. Xerxes escaped this particular plot; but fourteen years later he became the victim of another one within his palace.[44] Providentially, Mordecai was the one who discovered and reported the plot, for the record of his good deed was placed in the royal chronicles and later became the means of his exaltation (6:1-3). Xerxes was very concerned that loyalty to his throne be highly honored. In fact, Herodotus informs us that at one battle, "whenever he saw any of his own captains perform any worthy exploit he inquired concerning him; and the man's name was taken down by the scribes, together with the names of his father and his city" (8.90).

They were both hanged on a gallows. Compare the fate of Haman (7:10; cf. 5:14).

42. Gordis, "Studies in the Esther Narrative," p. 48.
43. Moore, *Esther,* p. 31.
44. Olmstead, p. 289.

3

HAMAN PLOTS ISRAEL'S DESTRUCTION

(3:1-15)

MORDECAI REFUSED TO BOW before Haman, whom Xerxes had elevated to the second position in the kingdom, and consequently Haman's wrath was aroused against Mordecai's nation. By means of the lot (*Pur*), the fateful day was determined for the destruction of Israel, and Haman promised to the king all the confiscated property. Haman then announced the day of Israel's destruction in letters in the king's name sent to the entire empire.

1. After these events King Ahasuerus promoted Haman, the son of Hammedatha the Agagite. The ominous events of this chapter occurred more than four years after Esther became queen (cf. 2:16; 3:7). By now Haman the Agagite had become the king's favorite courtier. The fact that he is introduced here as an "Agagite" has caused many modern scholars to question the historicity of the account, for it would seem highly improbable that a descendant of an Amalekite king executed by Samuel in Palestine nearly half a millennium earlier (1 Sam. 15:8; cf. Num. 24:7) could turn up here as a Persian official. A century ago C. F. Keil cautioned that "the name Agag is not sufficient for the purpose [of identification], as many individuals might at different times have borne the name Agag, i.e., the fiery."[1] But the problem was already solved, for Jules Oppert published an inscription from the time of Sargon of Assyria (c. 725 B.C.) that mentioned Agag as a place in Media (which later was incorporated into the Persian Empire).[2] "In the light of this evidence, it is apparent that Haman was a native of this province (rather than a descendant of the Amalekite king, Agag, as late Jewish tradition has supposed)."[3]

2. But Mordecai neither bowed down nor paid homage. It is not altogether clear from the text why Mordecai refused to bow before Haman. Even though he was a Jew and by now had admitted it to the king's servants (3:4), it must be remembered that "the custom of falling down to earth before an exalted personage, and especially before a king, was customary among Israelites; cf. 2 Sam. 14:4, 18:28, 1 Kings 1:16."[4]

About 100 B.C., Alexandrian Jews, possibly in an effort to vindicate the spirituality of Mordecai (see the Introduction), put this prayer into his mouth: "You know all things; you know, Lord, that it was not because of insolence or arrogance or vanity that I did this, that I did not bow down before arrogant Haman; for I would have been quite willing to have kissed the soles of his feet for Israel's sake. But I did it in order that I might not put the glory of a man above the glory of God."[5] In support of this interpretation, we have a description by Herodotus of two heralds from Sparta who arrived at the court of Xerxes: "When they came to Susa

---

1. C. F. Keil, *The Books of Ezra, Nehemiah, and Esther,* trans. Sophia Taylor, Biblical Commentary on the Old Testament, by C. F. Keil and F. Delitzsch (1873; reprint ed., Grand Rapids: Eerdmans, 1950), p. 343.
2. Jules Oppert, *Les Inscriptions Assyriennes des Sargonides et Les Fastes de Ninive* (Versailles: 1862), p. 25.
3. Gleason L. Archer, *A Survey of Old Testament Introduction,* rev. ed. (Chicago: Moody, 1974), p. 421.
4. Keil, p. 343.
5. Carey A. Moore, *Esther,* The Anchor Bible (Garden City, N.Y.: Doubleday, 1971), p. 106. Or see Lewis B. Paton, *Esther,* International Critical Commentary (New York: Scribner's, 1908), p. 228.

into the king's presence, and the guards ordered them to fall
down and do obeisance, and went so far as to use force to
compel them, they refused, and said they would never do
such a thing, even were their heads thrust to the ground, for
it was not their custom to worship men, and they had not
come to Persia for that purpose" (7:136).

On the other hand, Mordecai had almost made it necessary for Esther to pay such homage (in contradiction to Ex.
20:5?) by insisting that she not disclose her national identity
(Est. 2:20). Furthermore, it seems probable that Mordecai
himself, after replacing Haman as the king's favorite a year
later (8:2), would be expected to bow down to the king regardless of the religious connotations some might attribute
to such an act. Although later writers have asserted that
"Persian kings assumed divine honours . . . no such claim on
the part of the kings is found in the Persian monuments."[6]
Daniel had no problem saying to Darius the Mede: "O king,
live forever!" (Dan. 6:21; cf. Neh. 2:3 for Nehemiah's homage to Artaxerxes). It is therefore preferable to conclude
that Mordecai's actions be seen "as an expression of Jewish
national spirit and pride rather than adherence to Exod. 20:
5."[7] For an analysis of Mordecai's personal character, see
the Introduction.

3. Why are you transgressing the king's command? "Were
the servants genuinely concerned for Mordecai's safety and
chiding him in a friendly way, were they merely curious, or
were they resentful of his 'superior' attitude toward Haman?
The Massoretic Text does not say."[8]

4. For he had told them that he was a Jew. From one
standpoint, this reveals a courageous spirit, for Mordecai
must have sensed that this could bring trouble to himself and
even to his people. But his disclosure could hardly have

6. Paton, p. 196.
7. Moore, p. 36.
8. Ibid., p. 37.

been for religious reasons (in the true sense of that term), or he would not have waited until this moment, nor would he have insisted that Esther hide her religion. God is not truly honored by a "silent witness." But the real question is whether Mordecai had been even a "silent witness" to Jehovah up to this time and whether he was truly an "open witness" henceforth (see the Introduction).

6. *Therefore Haman sought to destroy all the Jews, the people of Mordecai.* When Haman beheld Mordecai's stubborn refusal to bow to him (v. 5) and discovered that Mordecai's excuse was that he was a Jew, he determined to destroy (Heb. *l^{e}hašmîd,* occurring twenty-five times in the book) all the Jews in the empire. Was Haman's decision motivated by purely personal revenge?

> Certainly the terrible pogroms [Russian = "devastation"] against the Jews in Russia and Nazi Germany were motivated by a variety of conscious and unconscious reasons. Men have never lacked the capacity to deceive even themselves and to find "good" reasons for their evil deeds. Sweeping though the destruction was to be (see v. 13), it was not without parallel. Even in antiquity, without benefit of the terrible efficiency of twentieth-century technology, such thoroughgoing slaughter was possible. Bloodthirsty massacres were carried out by the Persians against the Scythians (Herodotus I.106) and against the Magi at the accession of Darius I (III.79). And as Ringgren has pointed out (p. 129), Cicero accuses Mithradates of Pontus of killing between 80,000 and 150,000 Romans in one day in 90 B.C. (*Oratio de lege Manilia* III.7). In our own century, Hitler almost succeeded where Haman failed.[9]

Beyond all of this, however, as in the prologue of the book of Job, must be discerned the cosmic interplay between the machinations of Satan and the gracious but mysterious

9. Ibid., p. 43.

purposes of our sovereign God. We may be sure that Jannes and Jambres did not oppose Moses in their own human strength (Ex. 7:11; 2 Tim. 3:8). Centuries later it was Satan (Heb. "the adversary," or "the accuser") who "stood up against Israel and moved David to number Israel" (1 Chron. 21:1), resulting in the death of 70,000 men of Israel. And only one generation before the time of Esther, the prophet Zechariah saw in a vision "Joshua the high priest standing before the angel of the LORD, and Satan standing at his right hand to accuse him" (Zech. 3:1). It is perfectly clear, then, that the titanic death-struggle of the book of Esther simply cannot be understood apart from the satanic purposes toward Israel which the general context of Scripture reveals (cf. 10:18—11:1; Eph. 6:12).

7. Pur, that is the lot, was cast before Haman from day to day and from month to month, until the twelfth month, that is the month Adar. "Consistent with the author's practice elsewhere of explaining foreign words and practices . . . he rightly uses here the well-known Hebrew word *gôrāl*, 'lot' (Isa. 34:17; Neh. 10:35; 1 Chron. 26:14; Psa. 22:19; Jonah 1:7; Prov. 18:18) to explain the foreign word *pûr*."[10] In a later article on "Archaeology and the Book of Esther," Moore states: "It is clear that the word *pûr* in Esther 3:7 and 9:24 represents the Babylonian word *pūru,* meaning 'lot,' and, secondarily, 'fate' (J. Lewy, *Revue Hittite et Asianique,* 5 [1939], 117-24)."[11] Leon J. Wood calls attention to the interesting fact that "M. Dieulafoy, who excavated at Susa [1880-90], discovered a quadrangular prism which has the numbers one, two, five, and six engraved on its sides. This no doubt was the type of die used in this determination."[12]

---

10. Ibid., p. 38.
11. Carey A. Moore, "Archaeology and the Book of Esther," *The Biblical Archaeologist* 38, nos. 3-4 (1975):76.
12. Leon J. Wood, *A Survey of Israel's History* (Grand Rapids: Zondervan, 1970), p. 409.

Haman had the astrologers and magicians cast this lot in such a way that during the course of a single day of casting lots (perhaps on a large calendar?) the exact day of the year which would be most propitious for the destruction of Israel could be determined. Although the text merely designates *the first month, which is the month Nisan,* as the time when the lot was cast, it is quite possible that this occurred on the first day of that religiously important month. "The beginning of the New Year was an especially appropriate time for Haman to resort to divination because, according to the Babylonian religion, at that time the gods also come together to fix the fate of men."[13]

The final outcome once again confirmed God's assurance to His covenant people that when "the lot is cast into the lap . . . its every decision is from the LORD" (Prov. 16:33). God's overruling providence was particularly evident in this case, for as the astrologers and magicians cast the lot concerning each subsequent day of the year, it fell upon the thirteenth day of the twelfth and last month, allowing plenty of time for Haman's plot to be overcome and a counterdecree to be issued. Professor L. H. Brockington of the University of Oxford scoffs at the whole idea: "Who would plan a vindictive attack on the Jewish residents and then allow eleven months to elapse before its execution, or, when the tables were turned, who would expect the Jews to wait patiently until the thirteenth of Adar?"[14] The answer is that British and American attitudes about life cannot be automatically extrapolated into the ancient Near East, where it was unthinkable to ignore the guidelines of astrology, whatever the cost. Thus, Nebuchadnezzar's great decision to attack Jerusalem in 588 B.C. was determined by several forms of divination (Ezek. 21:21), including hepatoscopy, which

13. Moore, *Esther,* p. 38.
14. L. H. Brockington, *Ezra, Nehemiah, and Esther,* The Century Bible (London: Nelson, 1969), p. 217.

is divination by examining the liver of a sacrificed sheep.[15]

8. There is a certain people scattered and dispersed among the peoples in all the provinces of your kingdom; their laws are different from those of all other people. Moore translates: *"scattered, yet unassimilated,"* and points out that "the first participle refers to the Jews' being scattered throughout the hundred and twenty-seven provinces of the empire, while the second participle refers to their self-imposed separateness, or exclusiveness, a practice which helped them to preserve their religious and ethnic identity."[16] The uniqueness of Israel's moral, civil, and ceremonial laws has always caused offense to important elements of the Gentile world. Thus, Balaam bore unwilling testimony that it is "a people who dwells apart, and shall not be reckoned among the nations" (Num. 23:9). Moses asked his people: "What great nation is there that has statutes and judgments as righteous as this whole law which I am setting before you today?" (Deut. 4:8; cf. 32:31). It is possible that Haman did not actually name the subculture he was maligning for fear that Xerxes would remember decrees in the Jews' favor which had been issued by Cyrus and Darius Hystaspes (Ezra 1:1-4; 6:3-5; 6:8-12). Whatever his motive, "by slyly omitting the name of the people involved, Haman himself unwittingly set the stage further for Esther's unexpected opposition and her victory over him."[17]

They do not observe the king's laws. The mere fact that the Jews had unique customs could not have been an adequate cause for their destruction, for the Persian Empire was a veritable patchwork of cultural diversity. Haman knew this, and he therefore found it essential to misrepresent the Jews as a rebellious and dangerous element within the empire.

15. See J. S. Wright and K. A. Kitchen, "Magic and Sorcery," in J. D. Douglas, ed., *The New Bible Dictionary* (London: Inter-Varsity, 1962), pp. 766-71.
16. Moore, *Esther,* p. 39.
17. Ibid., p. 38.

Similar accusations were leveled at Christ Himself (cf. Luke 23:2) and the early Christians (Acts 16:20-21; 24:5). It was in anticipation of this very danger that God led Jeremiah to admonish the Jews who had been exiled to Babylonia: "Seek the welfare of the city where I have sent you into exile, and pray to the LORD on its behalf; for in its welfare you will have welfare" (Jer. 29:7). It is true that the Jews refused to worship mere creatures (cf. Dan. 3:12; 6:10), but to say that they did not obey "the king's laws" was a diabolical, perversion of the facts for the sake of personal gain.

9. I will pay ten thousand talents of silver into . . . the king's treasuries. Playing also on the king's greed, Haman offered to pay a vast sum of money to the royal treasury. Doubtless Haman was already a very wealthy man (see Herodotus 1.192 for the wealth of one Persian governor). Nevertheless, ten thousand talents was a fabulous sum, equivalent to about two-thirds of the annual income of the entire empire (cf. Herodotus 3.95). Verse 13 implies that the possessions of the Jews were to be confiscated by their Gentile neighbors, but we may be sure that Haman had effective plans for obtaining the bulk of their wealth.

Although the Jews were, of course, completely impoverished when they were exiled to Babylon by Nebuchadnezzar in 597 and 586 B.C., it is quite significant that many were able to give generously to their brethren who returned to Palestine under Zerubbabel in 537 B.C. (Ezra 1:4). In fact, it must have been their growing prosperity in Babylonia that deterred the great majority of the exiles from returning to the desolations of their homeland.

If the material prosperity of Jews was on the increase during the early Achaemenid period (beginning in 539 B.C. with the fall of Babylon under Cyrus), it must have accelerated rapidly in the final years of Xerxes (died 465 B.C.). Of great significance in this connection is the discovery (in 1893) of an archive of Murashû Sons of Nippur (a wealthy firm of bankers and brokers) consisting of 730 tablets from the period immediately following the time of Xerxes. "Ever since their discovery, these texts have attracted the interest of Biblical scholars because of the more than one hundred Jewish names found among the clients, customers, and business friends of the firm Murashû Sons. Jews . . . appear as contracting parties, as officials, as agents, as servants, and as witnesses. They are not only found in great number, but deal in commodities and money of large amounts, and occupy offices of great trust in the respective communities, being met even as collectors of rent or taxes and as royal officials."[18] In fact, four of the debtors named in these tablets owed to one of Murashû's sons by the next harvest the enormous sum of 24,540 bushels of dates; and of these four, two were Jews (Zabdia and Beletir, sons of Barikkiel).[19]

The great change in the economic, social, and political status of the Jews during the time of Xerxes indicated by the Murashû tablets leads Professor Horn to conclude:

> It certainly is tempting to see in the office of Mordecai the cause for this change, for the Book of Esther does not only attribute "power and might" in the Persian realm to him, but also great popularity among the Jews, stating that "he sought the welfare of his people" (10:2-3). If this explanation is unacceptable or incorrect, another cause has to be found that explains how the Jews, who until recently had lived in captivity or slavery, had suddenly experienced such a great change in their social and economic status in Babylonia, but not in Egypt. . . . Since no other events of

18. Siegfried H. Horn, "Mordecai, a Historical Problem," *Biblical Research* 9 (1964):23.
19. For a more recent discussion of these tablets, with special analysis of the Jewish names, see Michael D. Coogan, "Life in the Diaspora," *Biblical Archaeologist* 37, no. 1 (1974):6-12.

that period are known which could have been responsible for this change, it is only natural to see in the stories of the book of Esther more than fiction, and not the products of the fertile mind of a Jewish novelist of the Maccabean period.[20]

10. The king took his signet ring from his hand and gave it to Haman. In ancient times the signet ring was very important, for it was equivalent to one's signature.[21] Xerxes later gave his ring to Mordecai the Jew (8:2, 8, 10), even as Pharaoh had given his ring to one of the very first Israelites, who was likewise in a foreign court (Gen. 41:42). But in the present instance, the true character of Xerxes may be judged from the fact that he did not even bother to ask which nation was about to be destroyed! *The enemy of the Jews.* In the light of Genesis 12:3 this is an ominous descriptive title; it is repeated in Esther 8:1; 9:10, 24 (cf. 7:6).

11. The silver is yours, and the people also, to do with them as you please. Xerxes was capable of great generosity (cf. Herodotus 7.28). Moore suggests, however, that he really did accept the money, but not without an initial protest like Ephron to Abraham (Gen. 23:7-18). "The Greek translation of 3:11, 'Keep the money!' sounds very much like an initial stage in typical Near Eastern bargaining. . . . Mordecai expressly states that the money would go into the king's treasury in 4:7; and Esther's word 'sold' in 7:4 certainly suggests the same."[22]

12. Then the king's scribes were summoned. These were "stenographers and copyists (Herodotus 7:100, 8:90), not the professional class of learned scribes (cf. Jer. 36:26, 32)."[23]

20. Horn, pp. 24-25.
21. See various Bible dictionary articles under "Seal."
22. Moore, *Esther,* p. 40.
23. Ibid., p. 41.

The thirteenth day of the first month. It has been calcu-
lated that this was April 17, 474 B.C., because the first of
Nisan fell on April 5 that particular year.[24] The marvels of
God's providential control of every event in the unfolding
crisis cannot be ignored. The fact that the lot fell upon a
date exactly eleven months later (cf. Est. 3:13—March 7,
473) gave time not only for the decree to go forth but also
for the Jews to defend themselves successfully under the direction of a counterdecree issued more than two months
later (8:9). Surely the nation of Israel could say as David
had said half a millennium earlier: "My times are in Thy
hand; deliver me from the hand of my enemies, and from
those who persecute me" (Ps. 31:15). See my comments
on verse 7.

*13. Letters were sent by couriers to all the king's prov-
inces.* For comments on the Persian postal system, see my
remarks at 1:22.

To destroy, to kill, and to annihilate all the Jews. "The use
of three synonyms probably represents the legal device of being as specific and precise as possible in order to avoid confusion and uncertainty."[25]

In one day, the thirteenth day of the twelfth month. This
was the month Adar (v. 7), and the date was March 7, 473.
See my comments on verse 12.

And to seize their possessions as plunder. All who helped
to exterminate the Jews would gain spoil, but a portion of
the spoil would probably be turned over to Haman (cf. my
note on v. 9).

14. That they should be ready for this day. Carey A.
Moore, a representative of the liberal viewpoint, asks why
Haman sent out his decree eleven months in advance of the
proposed day of slaughter. After referring to one absurd

24. Cf. R. A. Parker and W. H. Dubberstein, *Babylonian Chronology 626* B.C.-
A.D. *75* (Providence, R.I.: Brown U., 1956), p. 31.
25. Moore, *Esther*, p. 41.

suggestion, Moore simply gives up on the matter: "This problem of the day, like so many other problems in Esther, is grounded in literary rather than in historical considerations, that is, the author needed time for his story's denouement."[26] However, C. F. Keil's suggestion of a century ago is still worthy of consideration: "the motive seems to have been . . . to cause many Jews to leave their property and escape to other lands, for the sake of preserving their lives. Thus Haman would obtain his object. He would be relieved of the presence of the Jews, and be able to enrich himself by the appropriation of their possessions."[27] Ultimately, of course, the question can only be resolved by a profound recognition of God's providence, which trapped the superstitious Haman in the machinery of astrology and thus provided the Jews the time they needed to seek and to find God's unforgettable solution to their dilemma (cf. my comments on v. 7).

15. While the king and Haman sat down to drink, the city of Susa was in confusion. "The incident closes with a brilliant dramatic contrast: on the one hand the nonchalant king and courtier with their wine; on the other the people of the city, apprehensive at the publication of so arbitrary an edict."[28] Doubtless the Jews had in this capital city many friends (cf. 8:15) who were stunned by this shocking example of irresponsible despotism. After the Jews, who else might be thus consigned to destruction at the whim of Xerxes?

26. Ibid., p. 43.
27. Keil, p. 348.
28. J. G. Baldwin, "Esther," in Donald Guthrie and Alec Motyer, eds., *The New Bible Commentary: Revised* (Grand Rapids: Eerdmans, 1970), p. 417.

4

ESTHER'S DECISION

(4:1-17)

MORDECAI'S GREAT MOURNING provoked the curiosity of Esther, who then learned from him of the decree and of his desire that she appeal to the king. When she protested that this might prove fatal to her, Mordecai insisted that it was her solemn responsibility to her people. She promised to go to the king if Mordecai would support her by a three-day fast.

1. When Mordecai learned all that had been done. Not only did Mordecai know what was publicly announced and have in his possession "a copy of the text of the edict" (v. 8), but he also knew of the agreement between Haman and the king and the exact amount of the money that had been promised (v. 7). This aggravated his grief, for he probably realized that it was the divulging of his nationality (3:4) that had brought Haman's wrath on his people. It was possibly through friendly eunuchs whom he had met at the king's gate (2:19, 21) that he obtained this important information.

He tore his clothes, put on sackcloth and ashes, and . . . wailed loudly and bitterly. For many centuries this act had served (in the Bible primarily, but cf. also Herodotus 8.99) as a sign of mourning, lamentation for personal or national disaster, penitence for sins, or special prayer for deliverance.[1] Even Old Testament saints looked at death with a certain fear and apprehension (Heb. 2:15). It was the bodily resurrection of our Lord Jesus that brought to full light for the first time "life and immortality . . . through the gospel" (2 Tim. 1:10). It is not at all certain that Mordecai was a true believer, however, for his mourning "need no more be interpreted as proof of deep religious faith than the presence of an officiating clergyman at an American funeral means the deceased was a 'believer.' "[2] In the New Testament, actions like Mordecai's were more a sign of unbelief than of faith (cf. Mark 5:38; 1 Thess. 4:13).

2. *No one to enter the king's gate clothed in sackcloth.* This is not surprising, given the shallowness of spiritual and emotional life in the royal court of Persia. The sight of sorrow might easily upset the fickle monarch. Thirty years later, Nehemiah had good reason to be "very much afraid" when Artaxerxes I challenged him in the royal court at Susa: "Why is your face sad though you are not sick? This is nothing but sadness of heart" (Neh. 2:2).

3. *There was great mourning among the Jews, with fasting, weeping, and wailing; and many lay on sackcloth and ashes.* In the Old Testament, prayer normally accompanied fasting, as in Joel 1:14 ("Consecrate a fast, proclaim a solemn assembly; gather the elders . . . and cry out to the LORD").[3] Thus, the fact that any mention of prayer is omitted in this time of crisis is deliberate and in harmony with the author's special purpose (cf. the Introduction). From the standpoint of the Israelite theocracy, therefore, the

1. Cf. W. Gordon Brown, "Ashes," in Charles F. Pfeiffer, Howard F. Vos, and John Rea, eds., *Wycliffe Bible Encyclopedia,* 2 vols. (Chicago: Moody, 1975), 1:159, and D. W. Deere, "Sackcloth," ibid., 2:1495-96.
2. Carey A. Moore, *Esther,* The Anchor Bible (Garden City, N.Y.: Doubleday, 1971), p. 47.
3. Cf. J. P. Lewis, "Fast, Fasting," in Merrill C. Tenney, ed., *The Zondervan Pictorial Encyclopedia of the Bible,* 5 vols. (Grand Rapids: Zondervan, 1975), 2:501-4.

situation is very different here from what it had been in
Hezekiah's day 250 years earlier, when, in an hour of national crisis, the king not only "tore his clothes" and "covered himself with sackcloth," but also "entered the house of
the LORD" and "sent . . . to Isaiah the prophet," requesting
that he "offer a prayer for the remnant that is left" (2 Kings
19:1-4). Nevertheless, even in unbelief (as is true of Israel
today), "from the standpoint of God's choice they are beloved for the sake of the fathers" (Rom. 11:28).

4. Esther's maidens and her eunuchs came and told her.
This and the following verses make it clear that these maidens and eunuchs were so isolated from general affairs in the
empire that they knew nothing of the decree that had electri-
fied the city.

Mordecai . . . did not accept them. By this means Mordecai apparently wanted Esther to understand that the calamity
was not merely personal, but that it was national as well.

*5. Esther summoned Hathach from the king's eunuchs,
whom the king had appointed to attend her.* Esther must
have trusted this particular eunuch in a special way, because
of the delicate task she entrusted to him. And Mordecai
must have trusted him too, for he divulged to him Esther's
true nationality and thus her dangerous position (cf. v. 8—
"for her people"). Could he also have been a Jew?

*6. So Hathach went out to Mordecai to the city square in
front of the king's gate.* "Literally, 'the broad place'; a traditional place for mourning (cf. Amos 5:16; Isa. 15:3; Jer.
48:38)."[4]

7. And the exact amount of money. Mordecai hoped that
when Esther learned what a vast sum of money was involved
she would see the urgency of obeying his command to plead
for her people before the king.

4. Moore, p. 48.

11. For any man or woman who comes to the king to the inner court who is not summoned, he has but one law, that he be put to death, unless the king holds out to him the golden scepter so that he may live. In order to protect themselves from unwanted intruders, Persian kings prohibited anyone from entering their private quarters unannounced or without a previous invitation. Herodotus allows only the exception of the seven benefactors who had assisted Darius in his rise to power in 522 B.C. (3.118, 140; cf. 3.72, 77, 84), but they were doubtless dead by now. Only the Bible preserves the law concerning the golden scepter, but that is sufficient to guarantee the historicity of such a law. Liberal theologians, of course, are incapable of accepting biblical testimony at face value on such matters: "Either the author was misinformed about Persian customs in this particular matter or, more likely, to increase the reader's suspense and appreciation of Esther's subsequent bravery, he deliberately exaggerated the dangers confronting her."[5]

I have not been summoned to come to the king for these thirty days. Esther's situation was especially precarious in the light of this month of neglect by the king. "As the queen of a polygamous and capricious monarch, who had not given a thought to her for a month past, she might receive even less sympathy than a stranger could expect."[6] Another has suggested that "had she requested an audience with the king, he would have denied it in order to avoid facing her and admitting that he no longer loved her. . . . Lest the idea that a mighty king should fear the emotional reactions of a mere woman seem too absurd, it should be noted that the great Xerxes did fear the wrath of his Queen Amestris (Herodotus IX, 109)."[7]

5. Ibid., p. 52.
6. J. G. Baldwin, "Esther," in Donald Guthrie and Alec Motyer, eds., *The New Bible Commentary: Revised* (Grand Rapids: Eerdmans, 1970), p. 417.
7. Moore, p. 49.

13. Do not imagine that you in the king's palace can escape any more than all the Jews. If Esther's national identity was not yet known in the palace, it is not clear at this point why she would have perished in the pogrom with other Jews unless Mordecai was referring to divine judgment (see v. 14).

14. If you remain silent at this time, relief and deliverance will arise for the Jews from another place and you and your father's house will perish. Impressed indelibly upon the heart and mind of every Jew was the divine promise through Abraham: "I will bless those who bless you, and the one who curses you I will curse" (Gen. 12:3). Nothing can be more obvious than the fact that this divine promise of protection for Israel and judgment for her enemies provided the background for Mordecai's statement, even though the divine name was studiously omitted by the author. (See the Introduction.) From what place could this kind of help have come? Surely not from some other nation or from a mere political power. Ancient Jewish sources (e.g., Josephus, the Lucianic recension of Esther, and the Targums) "are certainly correct to see in the Hebrew a veiled allusion to God."[8] For the same reason, Mordecai's threat concerning Esther and her father's house must be understood to be a threat of "divine punishment rather than mortal revenge by the Jews, the latter view being that of Josephus."[9]

And who knows whether you have not attained royalty for such a time as this? This may not have been Mordecai's original purpose for encouraging Esther to become Xerxes' queen, but it became suddenly clear to him in retrospect that God must have included all of these remarkable events within His sovereign and unfailing plan. This must, therefore, be recognized as Esther's moment of destiny. Mordecai's

8. Ibid., p. 50.
9. Ibid.,

plea was irresistible. The promises of God, the justice of God, and the providence of God shine brilliantly through the entire crisis, so that the mere omission of His name obscures nothing of His identity, attributes, and purposes for His chosen people and for the entire world of mankind. To believe that such a narrative could be the simple invention of a clever mind (as liberal critics consistently maintain) is to believe more than the facts can bear.

16. Go, assemble all the Jews who are found in Susa, and fast for me; do not eat or drink for three days, night or day. I and my maidens also will fast in the same way. There must have been a fairly large number of Jews in Susa, "since they were responsible later for killing three hundred men (9: 15)."[10]

Prayer to God is not mentioned here, but it is quite obviously implied, for mere fasting without the prayer that normally accompanied it (cf. my note on v. 3, and cf. Joel 1: 14) would have been useless under the circumstances. In fact, Moore suggests that her strict fast "made her, presumably, less attractive to the king."[11] The three days of fasting are to be reckoned inclusively, for it was on the third day (5:1) that the fast ended. A similar question centers on the exact interval between our Lord's death and resurrection.[12] Esther promised to Mordecai that her maidens would fast with her. Does this suggest that they were Jewish too, or at least that she had succeeded in teaching them something about prayer?

And thus I will go in to the king, which is not according to the law; and if I perish, I perish. The cry of aged Jacob, when he realized that he had no choice but to send Benjamin to Egypt with his brothers, must have been with a sense of

10. Ibid., p. 51.
11. Ibid.
12. Cf. James L. Boyer, *Chronology of the Crucifixion and the Last Week* (Chicago: Moody, 1977).

resignation to the inevitable: "If I am bereaved of my children, I am bereaved" (Gen. 43:14). Esther's words may have been more courageous (cf. Job 13:15; Dan. 3:17-18). Moore concludes: "Like all human beings, Esther was not without flaw; but certainly our heroine should be judged more by the brave act she performs than by the natural fears she had to fight against. The rash man acts without fear; the brave man, in spite of it."[13]

13. Moore, p. 53.

5

ESTHER'S FIRST BANQUET

(5:1-14)

THE KING GRACIOUSLY RECEIVED ESTHER, and she in turn invited him and Haman to a private banquet. At the banquet, the king offered to grant any request she might have, but she asked instead that they come to another banquet the next day. Haman was overjoyed at the special invitations, but he was chagrined at Mordecai's continued refusal to bow before him. Haman's wife and friends suggested that he have a gallows built and obtain permission from the king to hang Mordecai on it.

1. On the third day . . . Esther put on her royal robes and stood in the inner court of the king's palace in front of the king's rooms. During the approximately forty hours of fasting, God must have given Esther the necessary courage to present herself to the king unannounced. "Feminine strategy, as well as court etiquette, required that Esther not appear before the king in sackcloth."[1] *The king was sitting on his royal throne in the throne room.*[2]

2. When the king saw Esther the queen standing in the court, she obtained favor in his sight; and the king extended

1. Carey A. Moore, *Esther,* The Anchor Bible (Garden City, N.Y.: Doubleday, 1971), p. 55.
2. For a vivid picture of King Darius seated on his throne and holding his scepter during an audience at the palace at Persepolis, with Crown Prince Xerxes standing behind him, see James B. Pritchard, *The Ancient Near East in Pictures,* 2nd ed. (Princeton: Princeton U., 1969), p. 159, or Moore, opposite p. 22.

to Esther the golden scepter which was in his hand. This is surely one of the clearest examples in all Scripture of God's power over the hearts of kings to change their minds for the sake of His people. When *Abraham* came with Sarah to the kingdom of the Philistines, he was unnecessarily afraid that there was "no fear of God in this place" (Gen. 20:11). God *was* in control of that king. In spite of long delays, *Joseph's* pathway to power was paved by the providential interventions of God in the hearts of Potiphar (the chief executioner), the chief jailer, the chief cupbearer, and finally the Pharaoh himself (Gen. 39-41). *Daniel* lived throughout the long reign of Nebuchadnezzar (605-562 B.C.) and recorded the deep lessons this mighty monarch learned of the infinite power of Israel's God (cf. Dan. 2:47; 3:28; 4:1-3, 37; 5:21). Instead of death at the hand of Artaxerxes I, *Nehemiah* received the opportunity to express the desire of his heart and to have that desire satisfied (Neh. 2). But even a negative response from an earthly ruler is under God's hand, as illustrated by the Pharaoh whose heart was hardened by God against the requests of Moses (Gen. 5:1—12:36) and the hearts of the rulers whose rejection of our Lord Jesus Christ was according to "the predetermined plan and foreknowledge of God" (Acts 2:23). Whether for good or even for apparent evil (cf. Gen. 50:20), the ultimate encouragement of God's people is that "the king's heart is like channels of water in the hand of the LORD; He turns it wherever He wishes" (Prov. 21:1).

So Esther came near and touched the top of the scepter. Totally unaware of the divine impulse that changed his heart toward Esther, Xerxes the king extended to her the only means of her physical salvation. The spiritual application to the gospel message is remarkable. Because of our sin, we cannot enter the presence of an infinitely holy God. But this same God, in His incomparable love and grace, has provided a plan whereby even the worst of sinners may enter His presence and touch, as it were, His golden scepter. That plan involved the infinite price of our redemption paid by God's own Son upon the cross, whereby an open access to His throne of grace is now made available (Heb. 10:19-22). The illustration breaks down, of course, just at the place where our Lord's illustration of the importunate woman and the unrighteous judge (Luke 18:1-8) broke down, namely, the character of the ruler himself. The original text of the book of Esther offers no hints of her inward emotional reactions at this moment, but they must have been overwhelming. True to its character as a noninspired addition to the original text, however, the Greek translation (and Jerome's Latin Vulgate) adds the following vivid and entertaining insights:

> On the third day, when she had finished praying, she took off the clothing of a suppliant, and dressed herself in splendid attire. After she had called upon the all-seeing God and savior, she, looking absolutely radiant, took with her two maids, leaning daintily on the one, while the other followed carrying her train. She was radiant, in the prime of her beauty, and her face was assured as one who knows she is loved; but her heart was pounding with fear.

> When she had passed through all the doors, she stood before the king. He was seated on his royal throne, arrayed in all his splendid attire, all covered with gold and precious stones—a most formidable sight! Raising his face, flushed with color, he looked at her in fiercest anger. The queen stumbled, turned pale and fainted, keeling over on the maid who went before her. But God changed the king's spirit to gentleness. He sprang from his throne in alarm, and took her up in his arms until she revived. He comforted her with reassuring words, saying to her, "What is it, Esther? I'm your brother. Be brave. You're not going to die! This

practice applies only to our subjects. Come here!"

Then he raised his gold scepter and tapped her neck; he hugged her and said, "Now tell me all about it." "My lord," she said, "I saw you like an angel of God; and I was upset by your awesome appearance. For you are wonderful, my lord, and your face is full of graciousness." And as she spoke, she sagged with relief. The king was upset, and all his attendants tried to reassure her.[3]

3. Then the king said to her, "What . . . is your request? Even to half of the kingdom it will be given to you." Probably surprised at her unannounced appearance, Xerxes thought her request must be an urgent one. Even though his offer was a hyperbole (an intentional exaggeration for the sake of effect), it was never thought of as purely frivolous (he used the same offer in 5:6 and 7:2). Herodotus tells of a similar promise made by Xerxes at Susa to Artaynta, the bride of his son Darius, for whom he had suddenly developed a great passion (9.109). In similar fashion, Herod Antipas ("that fox" [Luke 13:22]) said to the beautiful daughter of Herodias: "Ask me for whatever you want and I will give it to you. . . . Whatever you ask of me, I will give it to you; up to half of my kingdom" (Mark 6:22-23). The results were even more disastrous for Herod than for Xerxes in the episode described by Herodotus.

4-8. And Esther said, "If it please the king, may the king and Haman come this day to the banquet that I have prepared for him." Esther's purpose in inviting the king and Haman to a private banquet in the first place was, of course, to accuse Haman of plotting to destroy her people, as she did the following day (cf. Est. 7:6). But now, perhaps sensing that she did not yet have sufficient influence with the king to make such a bold accusation against this powerful and honored statesman, she suddenly decided to postpone her re-

3. Cf. Moore, p. 108.

quest and to invite them to another banquet the following evening. If God can turn a king's heart like channels of water (see my comments on 5:2), He can do the same for a queen's heart. Marvelous indeed are God's ways with men, for the intervening events as recorded in chapter 6 provided the necessary demotion of Haman and the corresponding increase of Esther's confidence in God's direction in the course of events for her to accuse Haman openly at the second banquet.

On the other hand, the risks involved in postponing her request must not be underestimated either. As Moore points out, "her second refusal (v. 8) was tempting fate. Postponing her real request another time was a most questionable gamble; any number of things could go wrong in the interval between the two dinners: the king's benevolent mood could change, for example, or Haman could learn of Esther's true feelings toward him or of her relationship to Mordecai."[4]

9. *Then Haman went out that day glad and pleased of heart; but . . . was filled with anger against Mordecai.* This is a fascinating example of the deceived sinner, glorying in self and hating both the true God and His people. The psalms are filled with imprecations and prophecies concerning such. Although Esther's attendants knew of her relation to Mordecai (cf. my note on 4:4-8), Haman obviously did not. This ignorance of one vital fact proved, in God's perfect providence and justice, to be his undoing. "Despite the king's edict consigning Mordecai and all his people to destruction, Mordecai gave no outward sign of recognition to the author of all his troubles, not by even the flicker of recognition acknowledging his presence (cf. Job 28:7 ff.), let alone trembling before him. Mordecai simply remained seated at his accustomed place at the King's Gate (2:19 *et passim*), in his regular clothes (4:2), as if nothing had happened."[5]

4. Ibid., p. 87.
5. Ibid., p. 60.

11. Haman recounted to them the glory of his riches, and the number of his sons. Haman had ten sons (9:7-10). To have many children was considered to be a great honor not only in Israel (cf. Ps. 127:3-5) but also in Persia. Herodotus informs us, concerning the Persians, for example, that "next to prowess in arms, it is regarded as the greatest proof of manly excellence, to be the father of many sons. Every year the king sends rich gifts to the man who can show the largest number: for they hold that number is strength" (1.136).

13. Yet all of this does not satisfy me every time I see Mordecai the Jew sitting at the king's gate. "The memory of Mordecai's defiance was the only barrier to his complete satsifaction; in this Haman is true to type, for it is the lesser men who exaggerate slights, while the great can afford to overlook them."[6] "Just as a small coin held too closely to the eye can block out the entirety of the sun, so Haman's preoccupation with revenge blocked out for him all his other blessings."[7]

14. Have a gallows fifty cubits high made and in the morning ask the king to have Mordecai hanged on it. This gallows would be seventy-five feet high, quite a structure to be erected in one night, as liberal's delight to point out. But even Moore admits that it is "an obvious exaggeration *unless* the gallows was erected 'on some high structure' (so Hoschander, p. 205) or hill, so that all could see it."[8] Furthermore, we must not limit the power of a fabulously wealthy and jealous politician. The suspense has now reached the ultimate—"Esther has not yet spoken to the king about the pogrom; the king still does not know Mordecai saved his life; and now a gallows has been set up for Mordecai. Never have things looked worse!"[9]

6. J. G. Baldwin, "Esther," in Donald Guthrie and Alec Motyer, eds., *The New Bible Commentary: Revised* (Grand Rapids: Eerdmans, 1970), p. 418.
7. Moore, p. 61.
8. Ibid., p. 60, italics added.
9. Ibid., p. 61.

6

HAMAN HUMILIATED BEFORE
MORDECAI

(6:1-14)

UNABLE TO SLEEP THAT NIGHT, the king had the official chronicles read to him, and it was those records that told him of Mordecai's unrewarded loyalty in exposing a plot against the king. When Haman arrived at the court to ask for Mordecai's death, he was asked what honors should be bestowed upon a favorite of the king. Thinking of himself, Haman suggested a very elaborate form of exaltation, only to be told that he had to do those honors to Mordecai the Jew! When Haman arrived home, his wife and friends warned him that if Mordecai was indeed a Jew, his own doom was surely sealed.

1. *During that night the king could not sleep.* Was it increasing anxiety over the possible enormousness of Esther's request that kept the king awake? Or could it have been overindulgence at the first wine banquet? Concern for the fate of Daniel in the den of lions kept Darius the Mede in such a state of tension that "sleep fled from him" (Dan. 6:18). God accomplishes some of His deepest work in the hearts of men as they lay awake upon their beds at night (cf. Job 4:12-16; Ps. 4:4; Acts 18:9; 23:11).

He gave an order to bring the book of records, the chronicles, and they were read before the king. The Persians were careful to keep accurate records of events that affected the empire and the royal house (cf. Est. 2:23). Thus, through a catalog system available in Babylon, Darius found in his branch archives in Ecbatana the original scroll that Cyrus had issued concerning the Jews (Ezra 6:1-2; cf. 4:15). A modern counterpart might be the *Congressional Record,* which would be an excellent antidote for insomnia! "The Heb. indicates that they kept on reading, evidently all through the night."[1]

2. It was found written what Mordecai had reported concerning Bigthana and Teresh. Among the thousands of items recorded each year in the official book of records of the Persian Empire, it is providence that borders on the miraculous that this particular (all-too-typical) harem intrigue of four years earlier was read at this very time and to this very person.

3. And the king said, "What honor or dignity has been bestowed on Mordecai for this?" "That Mordecai had gone unrewarded for saving the king's life was a reflection on the Persian king, for whom it was a point of honor to reward his benefactors (Herodotus 3:138-140; 5:11; 8:85; 9:107)."[2]

4. So the king said, "Who is in the court?" His carpenters having worked all night to finish the gallows, Haman arrived at the court early in the morning to ask the king's permission to have Mordecai hanged. But before he could make his special request, the king summoned him to the throne room to answer an important question. Apparently the king wanted to consult any statesman he could find at this early hour, and Haman "happened" to be the most available man

1. J. G. Baldwin, "Esther," in Donald Guthrie and Alec Motyer, eds., *The New Bible Commentary: Revised* (Grand Rapids: Eerdmans, 1970), p. 418.
2. Carey A. Moore, *Esther,* The Anchor Bible (Garden City, N.Y.: Doubleday, 1971), p. 64.

at that moment! "This verse well illustrates the author's . . . gift for irony: here the early bird is gotten by the worm."[3]

6. And Haman said to himself, "Whom would the king desire to honor more than me?" Here is a clear illustration of the text: "Pride goes before destruction, and a haughty spirit before stumbling" (Prov. 16:18; cf. 11:2; 18:12). For another "splendid example of dramatic irony" see 2 Samuel 12:1-7 (cf. 14:1-17), "where the question posed was by one who, unlike King Xerxes, was fully aware of its implications."[4]

8. Let them bring a royal robe which the king has worn, and the horse on which the king has ridden, and on whose head a royal crown has been placed. The fact that Haman was able to begin listing immediately all the honors that would be most highly esteemed in the Orient suggests that he had often meditated on this very possibility and was ready to give the answer should the king ever ask him! "Where your treasure is," our Lord once stated, "there will your heart be also" (Matt. 6:21). With the tragic example of Haman before his eyes, how vastly important it is for the Christian to heed the command of God: "Keep seeking the things above, where Christ is, seated at the right hand of God. Set your mind on the things above, not on the things that are on earth" (Col. 3:1-2).

It was not enough for Haman to wear royal robes and ride on a horse from the royal stables. He had to use things that the king himself had actually used. "Everyone would think the King himself was coming, for all the outward trappings of royalty which were to be used."[5] Such was the insatiable pride of this courtier, and we see in him an enormous deterioration of quality from the Joseph whom Pharaoh honored with his signet ring, appropriate garments, his second

3. Ibid.
4. Ibid.
5. Baldwin, p. 418.

chariot, and power second only to his own (Gen. 41:39-45).
Likewise in contrast to Haman were the David for whom
Jonathan "stripped himself of the robe that was on him . . .
with his armor, including his sword and his bow and his belt"
(1 Sam. 18:4) and the Solomon to whom David gave his
own royal mule to ride in appropriate dignity to Gihon for
the public anointing (1 Kings 1:33).

The crown was not to be placed on the head of Haman but
on the head of his horse. "We do not indeed find among
classical writers any testimony to such an adornment of the
royal steed; but the circumstance is not at all improbable,
and seems to be corroborated by ancient remains, certain
Assyrian and ancient Persian sculptures, representing the
horses of the king, and apparently those of princes, with ornaments on their heads terminating in three points, which
may be regarded as a kind of crown."[6]

9. *Let the robe and the horse be handed over to one of*
the king's most noble princes. What Haman intended to be a
supreme honor to himself turned out to be his total humilia-
tion! (See 6:10.) "The king . . . alone was ignorant of the
feud between Mordecai and Haman, and of the fact that
Haman's decree was directed against the Jews, and therefore
included Mordecai."[7] "While the skeptic may well call this
series of events 'luck' ('good luck' for Mordecai, 'bad' for
Haman), the religious person is more likely to call it 'Providence' or 'the hand of God.' "[8]

Lead him on horseback through the city square, and pro-
claim before him, "Thus it shall be done to the man whom

---

6. C. F. Keil, *The Books of Ezra, Nehemiah, and Esther,* trans. Sophia Taylor,
   Biblical Commentary on the Old Testament, by C. F. Keil and F. Delitzsch
   (1873; reprint ed., Grand Rapids: Eerdmans, 1950), pp. 360-61. For a
   photograph of a stone relief of such a crowned horse, see Plate 4 in Moore
   ("Stone relief showing a Chorasmian with his horse, from the east stairway
   of the Apadana at Persepolis").

7. Baldwin, p. 418.

8. Moore, p. 67.

the king desires to honor." Fourteen centuries earlier, Joseph, another Israelite, was thus honored when the Pharaoh "had him ride in his second chariot; and they proclaimed before him, 'Bow the knee!' " (Gen. 41:43). Some day the entire universe will bow down before God's unique Son, Jesus Christ our Lord (cf. Ps. 2:4-12; Phil. 2:10-11).

10. Take quickly the robes and the horse as you have said, and do so for Mordecai the Jew, who is sitting at the king's gate. Apparently the king discovered that Mordecai, his benefactor, was a Jew on the basis of the official records that were read to him during the night. But being a fickle and perhaps absentminded monarch, he failed to connect this fact with the decree he had recently issued commanding the extermination of the Jews (cf. 3:11)! In view of Xerxes' attitude in 3:15 ("while the king and Haman sat down to drink, the city of Susa was in confusion"), he had probably dismissed the entire pogrom from his mind in recent weeks. Whatever callousness and incompetence human rulers may exhibit, we have a God in heaven who keeps us before His mind continually (Matt. 6:25-34). In His infinite care for the citizens of His kingdom, He "will neither slumber nor sleep" (Ps. 121:4).

12. Then Mordecai returned to the king's gate. Belatedly but gloriously honored (will not this be true of all believers whose service for Christ has been overlooked by the world and even the church?), Mordecai returned to his former position at the king's gate. Those who had formerly accused him to Haman (Est. 3:4) perhaps sensed that they themselves were now in deep trouble, even though the official decree for the pogrom was still in effect. One wonders whether Mordecai was still clothed in sackcloth!

But Haman hurried home, mourning, with his head covered. "With his head covered as a sign of grief (cf. 2 Sam. 15:30, 19:4; Jer. 14:3-4; Ezek. 24:17 . . .), he returns home to lick his wounds and seek solace with his wife and friends."[9]

13. Then his wise men and Zeresh his wife said to him, "If Mordecai, before whom you have begun to fall, is of Jewish origin, you will not overcome him, but will surely fall before him." Haman's friends, who had formerly acted as his counselors of vengeance (Est. 5:14), now acted as "wise men," for they correctly predicted his downfall. The sudden change in Mordecai's fortunes made them realize, with a superstitious awe borne of careful observation of God's providential care for His people since the days of Cyrus the Great, that Haman's preliminary fall would not stop short of total destruction. Could it be that, like Balaam a thousand years earlier (Num. 23:9, 21, 23; 24:9, 17, 19), they spoke beyond their own wisdom? (Compare also Rahab's amazing testimony to the Israelite spies [Josh. 2:9-13].)

14. The king's eunuchs arrived and hastily brought Haman to the banquet which Esther had prepared. "Literally, 'they hastened to bring.' This emphasizes Haman's importance, not any supposed tardiness on his part. There is little justification for some scholars' view that as the result of Haman's humiliating experience in 6:11, he either had completely forgotten about his appointment with the queen or was reluctant to keep it. On the contrary, Haman needed just such a party to bolster his deflated ego."[10]

9. Ibid., p. 66.
10. Ibid., p. 69.

7

ESTHER'S SECOND BANQUET
(7:1-10)

AT THE SECOND BANQUET, Esther now asked the king for the preservation of her people from destruction and boldly accused Haman of being the adversary. Enraged at this discovery, the king went into the garden and returned to find Haman pleading with Esther for his life. Accusing him of attacking the queen, the king ordered Haman to be hanged on the gallows he had built for Mordecai.

1. Now the king and Haman came to drink wine with Esther the queen. "The hour of the party is not stated; presumably it would have been in the afternoon rather than in the evening since so much happened later that same day, namely, Haman was hanged (v. 10), and Mordecai was personally received by the king (8:1-2), all of which would have taken some time."[1]

2. And the king said to Esther on the second day . . . "What is your petition, Queen Esther? It shall be granted you. And what is your request? Even to half of the kingdom it shall be done." "Once he heard her request, he could, of course, still refuse to grant it; but, having offered such emphatic assurances on three separate occasions, he could hardly deny that he had really made such a promise. Thus the king had painted himself into a corner."[2]

3. Let my life be given me as my petition, and my people

1. Carey A. Moore, *Esther,* The Anchor Bible (Garden City, N.Y.: Doubleday, 1971), p. 69.
2. Ibid., p. 73.

as my request. The king was obviously ignorant of the true significance of the events that had transpired in the previous twenty-four hours; but Esther must have seen the significance and the providential direction of those events. On the other hand, she "needed all the reassurance she could get; . . . for her this encounter was still a matter of life and death. Once she revealed her ethnic and religious origins to the king, not to mention her opposition to the king's most powerful official, her future was most uncertain."[3] With a boldness bolstered by desperation, Esther now stated her petition (for her own life) and her request (for the life of her people), following the exact wording of the king's question in verse 2.

4. For we have been sold, I and my people, to be destroyed, to be killed and to be annihilated. At last, Esther had identified herself as a Jewess. She stated her plight in the exact terms used in the decree of 3:13, terms that had by now burned themselves deep into her memory and conscience. The term "sold," of course, refers to the price that Haman offered to the king in exchange for the privilege of destroying this unwanted people.

Now if we had only been sold as slaves, men and women, I would have remained silent, for the trouble would not be commensurate with the annoyance to the king. A literal reading would be: "although the enemy is not equal to the damage of the king " The Hebrew wording is not altogether clear to us today, but it may mean that the punishment of Haman for his crime would involve far less financial loss to the king than would the destruction of thousands of Jews. By contrast, however, Esther would have remained silent if the Jews had been sold as slaves, for this would doubtless have brought much initial profit to the king.[4]

3. Ibid.
4. Fr. U. Schultz, "Esther," ed. and trans. James Strong, pp. 77-78, in vol. 7 of John Peter Lange et. al., *Commentary on the Holy Scriptures: Critical, Doctrinal, and Homiletical,* ed. and trans. Philip Schaff et. al., 24 vols. (Grand Rapids: Zondervan, n.d.).

5. *Who is he, and where is he, who would presume to do thus?* "First the king's life was threatened (2:21-23) and now the queen's; small wonder he was so excited."[5] The response of Xerxes to this desperate plea was exactly what Esther, Mordecai, and hundreds of Jews in Susa had been hoping for. Learning for the first time that Queen Esther was a Jewess, Xerxes was suddenly overwhelmed by the thought that she and her people had been sold into destruction by an unalterable decree that Haman had issued with the king's signet ring. To be sure, the king had originally consented to Haman's plot without much personal deliberation (cf. 3:10-11); but it is difficult to imagine any monarch being so absentminded that he could not even remember who had been responsible for initiating an empire-wide pogrom only two months earlier (cf. 3:7 and 8:9 for the timing of these events). It would be far more flattering to Xerxes to assume that he purposely refrained from turning immediately on Haman in order that the utter wickedness of the deed itself might be brought into full light by Esther.

6. *And Esther said, "A foe and an enemy, is this wicked Haman!"* Step by step Esther built up her case to an emotional and psychological climax that was almost irresistible before she finally named the actual cause of all her sorrows—Haman himself!

7. *And the king arose in his anger from drinking wine and went into the palace garden.* "Regardless of what the king's reason for leaving the room may have been, and commentators have offered many explanations . . . the king's absence sets the scene for the incident which seals Haman's fate."[6] Actually, there is nothing mysterious about Xerxes' momentary retreat to the palace garden: "the king shows a very

5. Moore, p. 71.
6. Ibid.

usual reaction to stress in getting up and striding out of the room."[7]

But Haman stayed to beg for his life from Queen Esther, for he saw that harm had been determined against him by the king. Taking advantage of the temporary absence of the king, Haman began to plead desperately for his life to Queen Esther, realizing that he could now find no favor from the king apart from her intercession. Haman probably had no way of knowing that she had been temporarily out of favor with Xerxes, and even if he did know this, he had overheard twice the king's fabulous promise to her, "even to half of the kingdom." Thus he was utterly trapped between an enraged king and an offended queen.

Just one day earlier Haman had led a Jew in triumphal procession through the streets of the city, and now he was pleading with a Jewess for his very life! A vastly greater reversal will occur at the dawn of the millennial age, when "kings will be your guardians. . . . They will bow down to you with their faces to the earth, and lick the dust of your feet" (Isa. 49:23), and "the sons of those who afflicted you will come bowing to you, and all those who despised you will bow themselves at the soles of your feet" (Isa. 60:14; cf. 14:1; 45:14, 23).

8. Haman was falling on the couch where Esther was. Then the king said, "Will he even assault the queen with me in the house?" Desperate for his own life, Haman fell at Esther's feet (cf. 2 Kings 4:27; Est. 8:3) as she reclined upon one of the gold and silver couches (cf. 1:6) in the banquet room. Herodotus mentions among the booty the Greeks took from their Persian enemies after the battle of Plataea "couches of gold and silver daintily decked out with their rich covertures and tables of gold and silver" (9.82). The Persians, as well as the Greeks and Romans, reclined at

---

7. J. G. Baldwin, "Esther," in Donald Guthrie and Alec Motyer, eds., *The New Bible Commentary: Revised* (Grand Rapids: Eerdmans, 1970), p. 418.

meals, and many Jews adopted this custom in New Testament times (cf. John 13:23).[8]

"The king's response has been variously characterized by scholars—excessive, drunken, a cruel jest, unreasonable, and so on; but one must remember that in antiquity very strong feelings and strict regulations centered on the harem (cf. Plutarch *Artaxerxes* XXVII.1, 2 . . .). Had Haman knelt as much as a foot away from the queen's couch, the king's reaction could still have been justified."[9] The fact that Xerxes "was ready to put the worst possible interpretation on Haman's posture"[10] tells us something of the abysmal moral atmosphere of the royal Persian court in ancient times.

As the word went out of the king's mouth, they covered Haman's face. This "word" is not the question he had just asked, but a command to execute Haman which is not recorded in the text. "The LXX has 'he was confounded in the face'. . . . However, the Massoretic Text's reading seems quite intelligible and correct, even though there is no evidence outside the Old Testament that the Persians covered the heads of the condemned; for evidence of such a practice among the Greeks and Romans, see Curtius VI.8, 22 and Livy I.26:25 respectively."[11]

9. Then Harbonah . . . said, "Behold indeed, the gallows standing at Haman's house fifty cubits high, which Haman made for Mordecai who spoke good on behalf of the king!" And the king said, "Hang him on it." As usual, the unimaginative monarch simply follows the suggestions of his courtiers. Harbonah was one of the seven eunuchs whom the king had sent to bring Vashti to the great banquet (1:10). The very height of the gallows Haman had constructed (which many liberal critics have rejected as impossibly high)

8. Cf. R. K. Harrison, "Meals," in J. D. Douglas, ed., *The New Bible Dictionary* (London: Inter-Varsity, 1962), p. 799.
9. Moore, p. 72.
10. Baldwin, p. 418.
11. Moore, p. 72.

made it so conspicuous that it could be seen from the palace! "In addition to suggesting an appropriate way to execute Haman, Harbonah's observation also had the effect of introducing a second accusation against him, namely, that he had knowingly tried to kill a benefactor of the king. If there had been any uncertainty in the king's mind concerning Haman's fate, this ended it."[12]

David, the great psalmist of Israel, had doubtless seen similar situations in his own vast experience with wicked men: "In the net which they hid, their own foot has been caught. The LORD has made Himself known; He has executed judgment. In the work of his own hands the wicked is snared" (Ps. 9:15-16).

10. So they hanged Haman on the gallows which he had prepared for Mordecai, and the king's anger subsided. Some have accused Esther of being callous and cruel in not interceding for Haman and preventing his death. But Moore has well observed that until he was actually executed, "Haman was not defeated: he was a falling, not a fallen, enemy. He had lost a crucial battle, but he had not necessarily lost the war. Were Haman to survive this round, he might recover and score a knockout in the next. So long as an enemy as powerful and shrewd as Haman lived, he was a threat to Esther, Mordecai, and the Jewish community. To say here that Esther was merciless and unfeeling is to misinterpret the entire situation. Thus, while her heart might have prompted her to be merciful, logic and prudence restrained her."[13]

12. Ibid.
13. Ibid., p. 74.

8

MORDECAI ISSUES A COUNTER-DECREE

(8:1-17)

HAMAN'S PROPERTY and position were now given to Mordecai by Xerxes and Esther. But the king was unable to reverse his decree against the Jews, so he empowered Mordecai to issue a new decree to counteract the first. This was quickly done and the Jews were now permitted to defend themselves on the thirteenth of Adar, the date Haman had originally set for their destruction. This produced great rejoicing everywhere and many became Jewish proselytes.

1. On that day King Ahasuerus gave the house of Haman, the enemy of the Jews, to Queen Esther. "In accordance with the law already referred to (cf. 3:9), the property of Haman was confiscated by the king."[1] Compare Herodotus, who, having described the execution of Oroetes, the wicked Persian governor of Sardis, reported that "the treasures of Oroetes" were turned over to King Darius (3.129). Haman's property was given by Xerxes to Esther, "apparently as a compensation for her suffering. Although a generous gift, it was nothing compared to what Xerxes promised his mis-

---

1. J. G. Baldwin, "Esther," in Donald Guthrie and Alec Motyer, eds., *The New Bible Commentary: Revised* (Grand Rapids: Eerdmans, 1970), p. 419.

tress Artaynte if she would release him from an embarrassing promise (Herodotus 9:109-11)."[2]

And Mordecai came before the king, for Esther had disclosed what he was to her. Now that she had revealed her own nationality to Xerxes (cf. 7:4), Esther was happy and proud to present Mordecai to the king as her guardian and her cousin. "Since Mordecai was appointed prime minister, Esther must have indicated not only their blood relationship but also the quality of that relationship and the character of the man."[3]

2. And the king took off his signet ring which he had taken away from Haman, and gave it to Mordecai. And Esther set Mordecai over the house of Haman. The king had already delighted to honor Mordecai for exposing the plot against his life (6:6), so it was perfectly natural to give him his fabulously authoritative signet ring (by which Haman had consigned all Jews to destruction [3:10-11; cf. 8:8] and to appoint him chief minister of the empire (compare the experience of Joseph [Gen. 41:42]). Thus Mordecai became even more powerful than Daniel, who was made the third ruler in Babylon (under Nabonidus and his son Belshazzar) and then the third ruler in Medo-Persia (under Cyrus and Darius the Mede). "Once promoted to be grand vizier by the gift of the royal signet ring, and to be manager of Esther's estate, he came into all the prestige and authority that Haman had known."[4]

3. Then Esther spoke again to the king, fell at his feet, wept, and implored him to avert the evil scheme of Haman the Agagite and his plot which he had devised against the Jews. "Virtually all commentators err in regarding v. 3 as the beginning of a new scene; rather, v. 3 is best understood

---

2. Carey A. Moore, *Esther,* The Anchor Bible (Garden City, N.Y.: Doubleday, 1971), p. 77.
3. Ibid.
4. Baldwin, p. 419.

as continuing the scene introduced by v. 1."[5] In spite of Haman's death and Mordecai's exaltation, the Jews were still doomed to destruction by an irreversible decree—a decree that reached forth, as it were, even from Haman's grave. Therefore Esther's task was not yet completed. In verse 3 the general content of her petition is outlined, but in verses 5 and 6 her actual words are given.

4. And the king extended the golden scepter to Esther. So Esther arose and stood before the king. For the spiritual application of this gesture, see my comments on 5:2. Moore feels that this may have been "a sign of encouragement rather than clemency. There is no reason to limit the use of the king's scepter to only one function, that is, the saving of the life of one who enters the throne room unsummoned (4:11, 5:2)."[6]

5-6. Then she said, "If it pleases the king and if I have found favor before him and the matter seems proper to the king and I am pleasing in his sight." "Some scholars delete this phrase with the LXX as being needlessly repetitious and hence a gloss; but although admittedly repetitious, these two courtly phrases, which have not been used by Esther earlier, underscore the pressure she feels and applies to the king. She is by no means certain of gaining her request; thus she must apply every pressure and persuasion at her disposal to avoid failure."[7]

Let it be written to revoke the letters devised by Haman. . . . For how can I endure to see the calamity which shall befall my people, and how can I endure to see the destruction of my kindred? Esther is desperately concerned now for the fate of all Israel throughout the province, as may be seen by her use of the above-mentioned fourfold introductory formula, which emphasized her personal relationship to the

5. Moore, p. 82.
6. Ibid., p. 78.
7. Ibid.

king. Not fully understanding the intricacies of Medo-Persian law, she appealed directly to the heart of the king for mercy upon Israel and for the reversal of "the letters devised by Haman," being extremely careful not to place any blame upon the king himself for his part in Haman's deed. "Esther now goes back to what she had passionately started in 7:3-4, when she was interrupted by the king's outburst against Haman (7:5)."[8]

7. So King Ahasuerus said to Queen Esther and to Mordecai the Jew, "Behold, I have given the house of Haman to Esther, and him they have hanged on the gallows because he had stretched out his hands against the Jews."

"The king seems to encourage Esther, indicating his favorable disposition toward both her and the Jews by citing what he has already done for them."[9] Many of the ancient versions, following the Septuagint, delete the phrase "Mordecai the Jew" in this verse, assuming that Esther had returned to the king for a second and private interview (vv. 3-8). But the word "you" at the beginning of verse 8 is both plural and emphatic. Thus, the Hebrew text and Jerome's Vulgate translation of the Hebrew are correct in including Mordecai at this point. "Mordecai has been in the king's presence since verse 1, where he was made prime minister (v. 2), and has watched Esther make her very moving plea for her people (vv. 3-6)."[10]

8. Now you write to the Jews as you see fit, in the king's name, and seal it with the king's signet ring; for a decree which is written in the name of the king and sealed with the king's signet ring may not be revoked. Although he was very anxious to spare the Jews and thus Esther, Xerxes reminded Esther and Mordecai that no one, not even the king himself, had the power to reverse the unalterable laws of the Medes and the Persians. (See my comments on 1:19.) Again we

8. Ibid.
9. Ibid., p. 79.
10. Ibid.

are reminded of the similar plight of Darius the Mede when Daniel was flung into the lions' den and the stone was sealed with the king's seal (Dan. 6:17). Instead of the initial decree being canceled and thus the people being given the impression that the king was guilty of making hasty decisions, a second and similarly unalterable decree had to be issued which in effect would cancel or overcome the effectiveness of the first one. A more cumbersome and costly system can hardly be imagined—and all for the sake of the king's intellectual reputation!

9. *So the king's scribes were called at that time in the third month (that is, the month Sivan), on the twenty-third day.* This would have been June 25, 474 B.C. Since the first decree went forth on the thirteenth day of the first month, April 17, 474 B.C. (cf. 3:12), two months and ten days had now gone by, giving plenty of time for the Jews to experience the full anguish of their impending doom. Why it took so long for the second decree to be issued is not clear from the text, especially when the urgency of the matter is set forth so clearly in the preceding chapters. On the other hand, more than eight months remained before the enemies of the Jews would be officially permitted to destroy them (March 7, 473 B.C.), so it was more important to prepare the counterdecree carefully than to rush the matter. It is also important to recognize that ancient bureaucracies were capable of as much red tape and inefficiency as modern ones. Thus there is no reason to deny the accuracy of the dates given in the text. The month "Sivan" was equivalent to the Babylonian month *simanu,* which was equivalent approximately to our May-June.

It was written according to all that Mordecai commanded to the Jews, the satraps, the governors, and the princes of the provinces which extended from India to Ethiopia, 127 provinces, to every province according to its script, and to every people according to their language, as well as to the Jews according to their script and their language. The wording here is quite similar to the first decree (3:12), except that the Jews are specifically mentioned here as recipients of the second decree. This emphasis is in agreement with the stated desire of Xerxes (8:8).

10. And he . . . sent letters by couriers on horses, riding on steeds sired by the royal stud. In this verse there are several obscure terms that the Septuagint did not even bother to translate. But, "whatever may be the precise meanings of these technical terms . . . their general meaning is clear enough: these are fast, strong horses which could carry the important message throughout the far-flung empire in good time."[11] Compare verse 14 ("the couriers, hastened and impelled . . ."). See my comments on 1:22 concerning the Persian postal system.

11. In them the king granted the Jews who were in each and every city the right to assemble and to defend their lives, to destroy, to kill, and to annihilate the entire army of any people or province which might attack them, including children and women, and to plunder their spoil. It was essential that the Jews be given plenty of advance notice to plan a defense against their enemies (cf. 8:13—"so that the Jews should be ready for this day to avenge themselves on their enemies"). "Had the Jews not assembled until the day of slaughter, such action would have come too late and availed them little."[12] The best defense is sometimes a tactical offense, so the expression "defend their lives" apparently was intended to be somewhat flexible. "The Jews must have played an aggressive, offensive role rather than a stubborn, defensive one (cf. 9:13 and 15) since 75,000 of their enemies fell in battle."[13]

11. Ibid., p. 80.
12. Ibid.
13. Ibid.

Some commentators have been shocked that Mordecai would issue a decree that involved plundering material possessions, to say nothing of instigating the death of "children and women." The answer seems to be twofold. In the first place, the very purpose of this decree was to counteract the first decree point by point (cf. 3:13) so that the Jews would not be left to any disadvantage at the hands of their enemies. But even more important, Mordecai and Esther were not Christians, and Israel was not identical to the church. It is totally unbiblical to judge the actions of ancient Israelites (such as Joshua in his destruction of Jericho [Josh. 6:21]) by the standards God has established for His bride, the church (cf. Rom. 12:14-21). The judgments that Israelites under Moses, Joshua, the judges, and the kings brought upon Gentile nations were actually divine judgments accomplished through that chosen nation (cf. Deut. 31:3-5), and this will yet again be true at the end of this age (cf. Mic. 5:7-9; Zech. 12:1-9; 14:14). If God has chosen to use Israel occasionally as a destructive instrument against those who reject the true God and has chosen to use the church as a peaceful instrument to call out a people for His name from among the nations (Acts 15:14), that is His sovereign and righteous decision. One divine action and method is no more or less spiritual than the other.

There may be progress of doctrine in the Scriptures, but there is no progression from error to truth. All Scripture is inerrant, and all Scripture is authoritative according to specific revelatory time-units, or dispensations. Mordecai and Esther were Jews, but not necessarily regenerate ("remnant") Jews. They were members of the Old Testament theocratic kingdom of Israel (like all Jews before the day of Pentecost) and thus enjoyed many of the privileges of Israelite citizens, even though they may not have been justified before God like faithful Abraham and were on the outward

fringes of the theocracy. One thing must be clearly maintained, however. They were not members of the body of
Christ and did not have the high privileges that this spiritual
organism alone possesses.[14]

Thus it is beside the point to suggest that the offending
phrase "children and women" be deleted as a gloss or to insist that only children and women who attacked Jews would
be killed.[15] This does not solve the problem of the book of
Esther. The world of our own day is being treated to a remarkably similar spectacle of retaliatory acts against ter-
rorists by an Israel that is fully supplied with "Esthers" and
"Mordecais" who are fanatically zealous for their nation
(and even for their religion) without being Christian or even
qualifying as the type of spiritual believers represented in
the Hebrews 11 hall of fame. Unless such biblical distinc-
tions are made, the book of Esther is in danger of being re-
duced to a subspiritual and therefore noncanonical status
(see the Introduction). To be consistent with such an
approach, other Old Testament books would have to be
dropped from the canon and the estimate of the Old Testament given by our Lord would be completely nullified (cf.
Matt. 5:18; 22:29; Luke 16:31; 24:25; John 5:46-47; 10:
35).

One possible interpretation of the offending phrase ("including children and women"), however, deserves consideration, especially in view of the fact that the author of the
book of Esther emphasizes the restraint exercised by the
Jews with regard to the spoil of their enemies (Est. 9:10, 15,
16). Robert Gordis insists that the verse should be translated: "By these letters the king permitted the Jews in every
city to gather and defend themselves, to destroy, kill, and
wipe out every armed force of a people or province attack-

---

14. Cf. Alva J. McClain, *The Greatness of the Kingdom* (Winona Lake, Ind.:
    BMH Books, 1959), pp. 325-30, 423-41.
15. Cf. Moore, p. 80, for documentation, and p. 83 for his own evaluation.

ing 'them, their children and their wives, with their goods as booty.' " Gordis explains that "the last five words in the Hebrew text of 8:11 are not a *paraphrase* of 3:13, giving the Jews permission to retaliate in precisely the manner planned by Haman, but a *citation* of Haman's original edict, against which its intended victims may now protect themselves. In accordance with modern usage, the citation should be placed in quotation marks. The book, therefore, underscores that, while the Jews were now empowered to fight against those who 'sought to do them harm' (9:2), their only goal was to repulse those who might attack them, their wives, and their children."[16]

14. The couriers, hastened and impelled by the king's command, went out, riding on the royal steeds; and the decree was given out in Susa the capital. It has often been observed that this provides a remarkably cogent illustration of missionary work today. God's death sentence hangs over a sinful humanity, but He has also commanded us to hasten the message of salvation to every land (cf. Prov. 24:11). Only by a knowledge of, and a response to, the second decree of saving grace through the Lord Jesus Christ can the terrible effects of the first decree of universal condemnation for sin be averted.

15. Then Mordecai went out from the presence of the king in royal robes of blue and white, with a large crown of gold and a garment of fine linen and purple. The word "crown" should be translated "turban," which was a "headdress to be distinguished from the royal crown (*keter*) of 1:11, 2:17, 6:8."[17] Blue and white were royal colors in the Persian empire (cf. 1:6, ASV). These were probably Mordecai's own official robes as prime minister rather than the

16. Robert Gordis, "Studies in the Esther Narrative," *Journal of Biblical Literature* 95, no. 1 (March 1976):52.
17. Moore, p. 81.

special attire that had been granted to him on his previous
day of exaltation (6:8).

And the city of Susa shouted and rejoiced. In order to
assure the citizens of Susa that his new decree was indeed
genuine and that the Jews were indeed in the royal favor,
Mordecai may have called for a great public meeting in the
capital city so that people could hear the terms of the second
proclamation. Clothed in his official splendor, he must have
had an electrifying effect on the expectant crowd. Note the
intentional contrast between the joy of this occasion and the
confusion produced by the first decree (3:15). Moore specu-
lates that "the cheering of the Gentiles may have been more
of an expression of their dislike and rejection of Haman than
their approval of Mordecai."[18]

*16. For the Jews there was light and gladness and joy and
honor.* The term "light" used in this context is "a symbol of
prosperity (Psa. 27:1, 36:10) and well-being (Psa. 97:11,
139:12; Job 22:28, 30:26)."[19] No man's joy is quite so
great as the joy of one who has experienced and overcome
grief. Only those who have wept can completely understand
the fullness of hope contained in that promise: "He shall
wipe away every tear from their eyes; and . . . there shall no
longer be any mourning, or crying" (Rev. 21:4). "Weeping
may last for the night, but a shout of joy comes in the morning" (Ps. 30:5). What happened in Esther's day was a just
cause for rejoicing in Israel. But the best is yet ahead for
the redeemed remnant of that nation. "Arise, shine; for your
light has come, and the glory of the LORD has risen upon you.
. . . The LORD will rise upon you, and His glory will appear
upon you. And nations will come to your light, and kings to
the brightness of your rising" (Isa. 60:1-3; cf. vv. 19-20).

17. And in each and every province, and in each and

18. Ibid.
19. Ibid.

every city, wherever the king's commandment and his decree arrived, there was gladness and joy for the Jews, a feast and a holiday. The word "holiday" is "literally 'a good day'; cf. 9:19, 22. Here as in later Jewish usage, the phrase represents a religious festival."[20] This feast was in anticipation of the Feast of Purim, which was first celebrated eight months later (9:17-19). Even in Judea, we may assume, the impact of Haman's decree and Mordecai's counterdecree was fully felt, surrounded as it was by various enemies. Forty-two years had passed since the second Temple had been dedicated by Zerubbabel and Joshua through the encouragement of Haggai and Zechariah (Ezra 6:13-22; Zech. 4:6-10). By now, their voices had been silenced by death, and the community had sunk into the various sinful practices that shocked Ezra so greatly upon his arrival in 458 B.C. (Ezra 9:1-2). Were it not for the temporary encouragement Mordecai's decree brought to this isolated community of Jews in Judea, it is quite possible that their condition would have been even worse than what Ezra found it to be sixteen years later. For archaeological evidence, see my comments on 9:16.

And many among the peoples of the land became Jews, for the dread of the Jews had fallen on them. The verb translated "became Jews" appears only here in the entire Old Testament. In fact, one finds very little evidence of Gentiles becoming proselytes to Israel in significant numbers until intertestament and early New Testament times. Our Lord referred disparagingly to zealous Pharisees who traveled about "on sea and land to make one proselyte; and when he becomes one, you make him twice as much a son of hell as yourselves" (Matt. 23:15). Homer A. Kent explains our Lord's statement to refer not to "the God-fearing Gentile who stopped short of circumcision (i.e., proselyte of the gate), but the Gentile who had been persuaded to adopt

20. Ibid.

Judaism *in toto,* including all the traditions taught by such Pharisees. Proselytes made by these unspiritual Pharisees (and doubtless added to their sect) would merely add rabbinic traditions to their pagan notions."[21]

It is very clear from the book of Acts that many thousands of Gentiles had attached themselves to Jewish synagogues throughout the Roman Empire, not because of any "dread of the Jews" in the sense of Esther 8:17, but because of the vast superiority of Jewish religion and life-style to the increasing corruption and emptiness of paganism in all its forms. It was among such people that Paul found the most positive response to the gospel.[22] Israel had now begun to experience one of the greatest deliverances of God since the Exodus, and the lesson was obvious to many (cf. 9:2-3; Ex. 15:16; Deut. 11:25; Josh. 2:8-11; Neh. 6:16).

21. Charles F. Pfeiffer and Everett F. Harrison, eds., *The Wycliffe Bible Commentary* (Chicago: Moody, 1962), p. 970.
22. Cf. Louis Goldberg, "Proselyte," in Charles F. Pfeiffer, Howard F. Vos, and John Rea, eds., *Wycliffe Bible Encyclopedia,* 2 vols. (Chicago: Moody, 1975), 2:1418.

9

THE JEWS VICTORIOUS AND PURIM INSTITUTED

(9:1—10:3)

WHEN THE FATEFUL DAY ARRIVED, the Jews successfully defended themselves with the aid of government officials and slew 500 men in Shushan including the ten sons of Haman. Esther obtained permission for the Jews to defend themselves a second day as well, and 300 more enemies were slain in Shushan. In the provinces, 75,000 enemies were slain. The Feast of Purim was then established by special letters to commemorate this tremendous deliverance. A second letter confirmed the first and provided for a fast as well. Mordecai's greatness and his love for Israel were recorded in the chronicles of the kingdom.

1. Now in the twelfth month (that is, the month Adar), on the thirteenth day when the king's command and edict were about to be executed. Mordecai's counterdecree had gone forth on June 25, 474 B.C., and thus the Jews had most of that summer and fall, as well as the winter months, to prepare for this fateful day, March 7, 473 B.C. For Israel, it was a never-to-be-forgotten day in history, though secular historians almost completely ignore it.

111

On the day when the enemies of the Jews hoped to gain the mastery over them, it was turned to the contrary so that the Jews themselves gained the mastery over those who hated them. Here again, any reference to the providence of God is deliberately suppressed by the author (see the Introduction). A spectacular modern example of this principle of nearly total reversal is the 1967 war of the Arabs and Jews.

> Astounding was the only word for it. In 60 hours the war that exploded upon the Middle East became a fact of history. Tiny Israel stood in the role of victor over the surrounding Arab nations that had vowed to exterminate her. Middle Eastern alliances, balances of power, even political boundaries, were of a new shape, as though mutated by a Biblical cataclysm. Seldom in military history has victory been so efficient or so visibly decisive in so short a span of time. So swiftly did Israel mount her assault that her adversaries were deprived of the means of winning almost before the world awakened to the fact that a war was in progress. . . . The Israelis experienced an ecstasy which is given to few people of any generation to know.[1]

2. The Jews assembled in their cities throughout all the provinces of King Ahasuerus to lay hands on those who sought their harm; and no one could stand before them, for the dread of them had fallen on all the peoples. In this context, the expression "to lay hands on" means to kill (cf. 2:21; 3:6; 6:2). " 'Those who sought their harm' refers to those who would actually fight the Jews (cf. Num. 35:23; 1 Sam. 24:10, 25:26) and not to those who were merely hostile. Such an interpretation does not preclude the Jews taking the offensive in some instances rather than waiting to be attacked, since the Jews would have known who their more implacable enemies were."[2] It is easy to underestimate the

---

1. *Life,* June 16, 1967, pp. 33, 38a.
2. Carey A. Moore, *Esther,* The Anchor Bible (Garden City, N.Y.: Doubleday, 1971), p. 86.

hatred that multitudes of people throughout the empire sustained toward the Jews and thus to misunderstand the response of the Jews to their potential tormentors. Recent history vividly illustrates this enormous tension, from Nazi Germany to the state of Israel. "Judging from 9:2, 5, and especially 16, we must conclude that Haman's letter (3:13) had either created or fanned the flames of anti-Semitism throughout the empire and that, whether motivated by Haman's propaganda or their own greed, thousands of 'enemies of the Jews' (cf. v. 16) were eagerly awaiting the appointed day."[3]

3. *All the princes of the provinces, the satraps, the governors, and those who were doing the king's business assisted the Jews, because the dread of Mordecai had fallen on them.* The tenor of the second decree made it perfectly clear to Persian officials that the king, to say nothing of Mordecai his prime minister, now favored the Jews. To have joined in the attack against the Jews now would surely have brought wrath upon them sooner or later. Presumably this was not their first such choice between the "unchangeable" but contradictory decrees that issued from the mysterious throne room of the Persian monarch! Could they perhaps have recalled the horrible fate of those "commissioners and satraps" sixty-five years earlier (in 538 B.C.) who took advantage of the legal helplessness of Darius the Mede when they forced him to seal the stone on the lions' den with his favorite subordinate inside? Once the letter of the law against Daniel had been fulfilled, Darius the Mede was free to demonstrate his true feelings toward Daniel's enemies. "The king then gave orders, and they brought those men who had maliciously accused Daniel, and they cast them, their children, and their wives into the lions' den; and they had not reached the bottom of the den before the lions overpowered them and

3. Ibid., p. 90.

crushed all their bones" (Dan. 6:24). Politicians who plan
to survive in office for long find it expedient to mastermind
their superiors! "The author does not indicate what type of
support was given, whether moral, military, financial, or all
three. More significantly, he acknowledges the help of mortal men but says nothing about the Lord God of Israel, an
omission which is certainly deliberate."[4]

*5. Thus the Jews struck all their enemies with the sword,
killing and destroying; and they did what they pleased to
those who hated them.* Many Persian citizens took full advantage of the first decree to attack (legally) their hated
Jewish neighbors. Deprived of full government support and
faced by a zealous and newly encouraged people, they were
totally defeated. "The boast in verse 5 that the Jews did 'as
they pleased' suggests that some Jews, at least, were given a
free hand by the authorities and did not confine themselves
to self-defense; they may very well have sought out and
destroyed those who were hostile to them, that is, their clearly established implacable foes."[5] Thus, although the wording of this verse has proved to be highly offensive to many
people today, it must be understood in the light of the entire
context. See my comments on 8:11.

*6-10. And in Susa the capital the Jews killed and de-
stroyed five hundred men, and Parshandatha, Dalphon, As-
patha, Poratha, Adalia, Aridatha, Parmashta, Arisai, Aridai,
and Vaizatha, the ten sons of Haman the son of Hammedatha, the Jews' enemy.*

> The execution of Haman's sons was, of course, inevitable.
> They had lost their inheritance (8:1), but as long as they
> were alive they could still cause trouble for the Jews. Es-
> ther's request, however, that their corpses be publicly dis-
> played and the Jews in Susa allowed to fight again the next
> day (vs. 13) is much more problematic. . . . If the ene-

4. Ibid., p. 86.
5. Ibid., p. 90.

mies of the Jews had been decisively defeated and were willing to leave the Jews alone, then Esther's request would certainly be vengeful. If after the thirteenth, however, there were still in Susa pockets of resistance looking forward to a second round with the Jews, then Esther's request would be realistic and necessary, and the exposure and desecration of Haman's sons could be understood as a deterrent (cf. 1 Sam. 31:10, Herodotus 3:125, 6:30, 7:238) and not, as Paton has argued (I.C.C., p. 287), a case of her malignant spirit of vengeance pursuing them even after death.[6]

All the sons of Haman, with the possible exception of Adalia, had Persian names.[7]

But they did not lay their hands on the plunder. The Jews did not take advantage of their rightful privilege (cf. the decree of Mordecai [8:11]). This point is repeated for emphasis in verses 15 and 16 in order that the purity of their motives might be obvious to all. Haman's decree had included the plundering of Jewish possessions (cf. 3:13). "Such self-restraint as the Jews expressed here is quite prudent in a situation where a minority is essentially defending itself from its enemies rather than initiating the conflict. . . . Possibly the Jews also remembered Abraham's wise logic: he took no loot lest later on the people resentfully say, 'I have made Abram rich' (see Gen. 14:22-24)."[8]

12. And the king said to Queen Esther, "The Jews have killed and destroyed five hundred men and the ten sons of Haman in Susa the capital. What then have they done in the rest of the king's provinces! Now what is your petition? It shall even be granted you. And what is your further request? It shall also be done." Apparently the king actually rejoiced

---

6. Ibid., p. 91.
7. For root meanings of the names, see Fr. U. Schultz, "Esther," ed. and trans. James Strong, p. 90, n., in vol. 7 of John Peter Lange et. al., *Commentary on the Holy Scriptures: Critical, Doctrinal, and Homiletical,* ed. and trans. Philip Schaff et. al., 24 vols. (Grand Rapids: Zondervan, n.d.).
8. Moore, p. 88.

to hear that Esther's people had gained such a tremendous
victory in Susa, and he was now anticipating similar reports
from the various parts of his empire. "Although some of
those killed had probably been guests at the king's parties
(cf. 1:3, 5), he is concerned only with pleasing Esther, who,
he detects, is still not entirely satisfied."[9]

*13. Then said Esther, "If it pleases the king, let tomorrow
also be granted to the Jews who are in Susa to do according
to the edict of today; and let Haman's ten sons be hanged on
the gallows."* Although the Scripture does not specifically
state this, it seems appropriate to assume that Queen Esther
had learned of a Persian plot to attack the Jews of Susa on
the following day as well, and therefore she asked permission
for the Jews to defend themselves again. The king immediately saw the dangerous position the Jews (including his
queen) would be in if they were thus caught off guard, so he
issued a new decree permitting the Jews to kill their enemies
in Susa on the fourteenth (as well as the thirteenth) of Adar,
for Mordecai's decree had only specified one day for the Jews
to defend themselves in this manner (8:13). This additional
decree was obeyed (9:15) and 300 more enemy aggressors
were slain in Susa. Thus, the decree of verse 14 does not
refer primarily to the sons of Haman, but to the battle of
verse 15.

Not desiring to give Esther the benefit of the doubt here,
J. G. Baldwin, an evangelical commentator, suggests that the
queen "was extremely vindictive in asking for a further day's
slaughter in Susa. To respond to the grace of God by hatred
to men was particularly despicable."[10] Surprisingly, Moore,
a liberal writer, is more cautious: "It is Esther's request for
the exposure of Haman's sons and an extension of the fighting, as well as her 'failure' to intercede for Haman in 7:9,

9. Ibid.
10. J. G. Baldwin, "Esther," in Donald Guthrie and Alec Motyer, eds., *The
New Bible Commentary: Revised* (Grand Rapids: Eerdmans, 1970), p. 419.

that has been primarily responsible for her reputation as a sophisticated Jael, i.e., a deceitful and bloodthirsty woman (cf. Judges 4:17-22). . . . But unless one is willing to judge Esther's outward act in complete isolation, without any real knowledge of her inner motives and without full knowledge of the external circumstances, then one's judgment must be tentatively made.."[11] The ten sons of Haman had already been killed (cf. v. 10), so the purpose of hanging their dead bodies on the gallows was to warn the enemies of the Jews of the utter futility of attacking a people whose providential protection was already proverbial in Persia (cf. 6:13). At least from the time of Moses it was Israelite custom to hang the dead bodies of criminals to warn against similar crimes (Deut. 21:22-23; cf. Num. 25:4, ASV; 2 Sam. 21:6).

15. And the Jews who were in Susa assembled also on the fourteenth day of the month Adar and killed three hundred men in Susa, but they did not lay their hands on the plunder. "It is interesting that almost twice as many were killed in the acropolis [translated "the capital" in 9:6, NASB, but actually the royal part of the capital—a part that was separated from the rest of the city] as in the city, although the city was larger; this fact may justify exposing Haman's sons as a deterrent action. If revenge was the primary reason for the second day's fighting, the author gives no hint of it. He does not glory in details of the battle; concerning the fighting itself he simply states the time, place, and casualty figures."[12]

16. Now the rest of the Jews who were in the king's provinces assembled, to defend their lives and rid themselves of their enemies, and kill 75,000 of those who hated them; but they did not lay their hands on the plunder. This, of course, had occurred on the previous day, the 13th of Adar (cf. v. 17). There is no problem in the Hebrew narrative, for "it is possible to translate the verbs of v. 16 by the pluperfect,

11. Moore, p. 88.
12. Ibid.

and this makes better sense."[13]   Thus translated, the verses would read: "Now the rest of the Jews who were in the king's provinces had assembled, to defend their lives and rid themselves of their enemies, and had killed 75,000 of those who hated them; but they had not laid their hands on the plunder."   The Septuagint reduces the number 75,000 down to 15,000, but this change "must have come much later in the transmission of the Greek text, since 75,000 is supported by both Josephus and the Syriac, two versions based upon the Septuagint."[14]   When one considers the vast extent of the Persian Empire, the figure 75,000, though thought to be an exaggeration by some commentators, is perfectly reasonable in proportion to the 800 killed in Susa alone.

What effect did Mordecai's counterdecree have upon the enemies of the Jews in Palestine?   The Bible is silent on this fascinating question, but there is some archaeological evidence that the two centers of Samaritan opposition to the Jews, Samaria and Shechem, were destroyed about this time. "A positive relationship can be proposed between the lag in occupation early in the fifth century at Samaria, the destruction of Shechem dated ca. 475, and the fighting in the Persian empire dated early in 473 by the book of Esther. This event described in Esther provides, in turn, a possible historical explanation for these archaeological findings in Palestine that have hitherto gone unexplained."[15]

18-19. The Jews who were in Susa assembled on the thirteenth and the fourteenth of the same month, and they rested on the fifteenth day and made it a day of feasting and rejoicing. Therefore the Jews of the rural areas, who live in the rural towns, make the fourteenth day of the month Adar a holiday for rejoicing and feasting and sending portions of

13. Baldwin, p. 419.
14. Moore, p. 89.
15. William H. Shea, "Esther and History," *Andrews University Seminary Studies* 14, no. 1 (Spring 1976):244.

food to one another. As on our Christmas Day, gifts were exchanged (cf. Neh. 8:10, 12; and Rev. 11:10) and the poor were cared for (Est. 9:22). During the intertestament period, the fourteenth of Adar was called "Mordecai's day" (2 Maccabees 15:36, RSV). See my additional discussion under 9:26. "Modern Jews hold their festal meal towards the evening of the 14th, just a month before Passover."[16] "On one crucial point the author seems quite clear if not explicit: men, not Yahweh, delivered the Jews. It was the influence of Mordecai (vss. 3-4) and the preparations and prowess of the Jews themselves (vs. 2) that turned the tide of battle in their favor."[17] For a discussion of the viewpoint of the author of the book of Esther, see the Introduction.

20-21. Then Mordecai recorded these events, and he sent letters to all the Jews who were in all the provinces of King Ahasuerus, both near and far, obliging them to celebrate the fourteenth day of the month Adar, and the fifteenth day of the same month, annually. It is just possible that several months or even years had now passed. As Mordecai reviewed "these events" (that is, the events that occurred on the fourteenth and fifteenth of Adar), he issued a decree that there should no longer be two distinct holidays (the fourteenth in the provinces and the fifteenth in Susa), but that both days should be observed as the Feast of Purim (vv. 26-28). This decision may have been influenced by the fact that Jews throughout the provinces were beginning to observe both days when they heard what had happened in the capital city on the fifteenth of Adar (cf. 23).

25. But when it [literally, "she" = Esther?] *came to the king's attention, he commanded by letter that his wicked scheme which he had devised against the Jews, should return on his own head, and that he and his sons should be hanged*

16. Baldwin, p. 419.
17. Moore, p. 91.

on the gallows. Baldwin suggests that "verses 24 and 25 may be a quotation from Mordecai's letter following from the second clause of v. 23."[18] The author here telescopes all the major events of that remarkable year. It is true that Xerxes' published decree was through Mordecai and did not deal specifically with Haman or his sons. Furthermore, Haman and his sons were actually executed nine months apart. But it is not the author's purpose here to insult the intelligence of the reader by reviewing all the details. The basic fact is this: the king denounced the enemies of the Jews when the facts were made known to him, and this denunciation was official. It is refreshing to find Carey A. Moore dismissing this supposed contradiction with these words: "as with all difficult and obscure readings, many have called this a gloss."[19] Emending the text arbitrarily has always been a favorite standby for those who deny the absolute inerrancy of God's inscripturated revelation in the autographs.

26-28. Therefore they called these days Purim after the name of Pur. And because of the instructions in this letter, both what they had seen in this regard and what had happened to them, the Jews established and made a custom for themselves, and for their descendants, and for all those who allied themselves with them, so that they should not fail to celebrate these two days according to their regulation, and according to their appointed time annually. So these days were to be remembered and celebrated throughout every generation. The author's explanation that "Purim" derives from the word "Pur" (cf. my comments on 3:7) underscores the crucial importance of the casting of lots as an instrument in God's providential control of Israel's affairs in general and Haman's use in particular (cf. 9:24). There are over seventy Old Testament references to casting the lot (Heb.

18. Baldwin, p. 419.
19. Moore, p. 94.

gôrāl) before the time of Esther, the true significance of this act being stated in Proverbs 16:33—"the lot is cast into the lap . . . its every decision is from the LORD." Thus "Purim" was by no means an inappropriate name for the feast that celebrated the deliverance of Israel from the hands of her enemies.

About 161 B.C., Judas Maccabeus and his army defeated the army of Syria and killed its general, Nicanor. "They decreed that this day shoud be celebrated each year on the thirteenth day of Adar" (1 Maccabees 7:49, RSV). In the supplementary account written somewhat later, this celebration is described as "the day before Mordecai's day" (2 Maccabees 15:36, RSV), thus indicating that Purim was known to be celebrated on the fourteenth of Adar. Still later (c. A.D. 90), Josephus referred to the victory over Nicanor on the thirteenth of Adar: "the Jews celebrate this victory every year, and esteem it as a festival day" (*Antiquities* 12.10.5),[20] but he also insisted that Purim was celebrated the fourteenth and fifteenth of Adar, so that "even now all the Jews that are in the habitable earth keep these days festival, and send portions to one another" (*Antiquities* 11.6.13).

It has been objected that Josephus (following the Septuagint) used the word *"phroureas"* ("guard," "protect"), instead of *Purim,* but this cannot be considered significant. J. Stafford Wright observes that "Nicanor's Day was not observed after the 7th century A.D., but Adar 13 was gradually made part of Purim. As opposed to Adar 14 and 15, which were days of lively celebration, Adar 13 was a day of fasting."[21] See my comments on 9:31.

20. Both this quotation from Josephus' *Antiquities of the Jews* and the quotation immediately following it are from William Whiston's famous and accurate translation of Flavius Josephus, *Complete Works of Flavius Josephus* (1830; reprint ed., Grand Rapids: Kregel, 1970).

21. J. Stafford Wright, "Purim," in J. D. Douglas, ed., *The New Bible Dictionary* (London: Inter-Varsity, 1962), p. 1066.

Carey A. Moore makes a great point of the supposed contradiction between this passage (9:26-28) and 9:19, which states, in his opinion, that Jews "who live" (present tense) "in the villages and towns in the author's, or more likely a glossator's, own day" were observing only the fourteenth of Adar.[22] Moore at this point conveniently ignores his own later warning against labeling problem verses as glosses,[23] and insists that verse 19, "which implies a distinction between Jews living in walled and unwalled cities, is certainly a gloss, because it contradicts verses 21-22."[24] But a far more natural explanation is that verse 19 describes the initial response of Jews throughout the empire (the author being a contemporary and thus able to use the present tense to describe their actions), whereas the following verses (9:20-28) describe the later custom as a result of Mordecai's festal letter. Because this feast had not been anticipated in the law of Moses (cf. Lev. 23), it was essential that its status in the Jewish religious calendar be strongly, repeatedly, and officially confirmed.

29. Then Queen Esther, daughter of Abihail, with Mordecai the Jew, wrote with full authority to confirm this second letter about Purim. This is not the same letter as that which Mordecai himself had sent to the Jews concerning the obligation to celebrate the fourteenth and fifteenth of Adar (9:20). This is a second official letter, issued by Esther herself (the Hebrew verb translated "wrote" is feminine) but cosigned by Mordecai, to confirm his festal letter. (Moore agrees.[25]) Presumably there was still some resistance in the provinces to the idea of celebrating both days (cf. 9:19). Many scholars have denied the authenticity of 9:29-32, but

22. Moore, p. 89.
23. Ibid., p. 94.
24. Ibid., p. 89.
25. Ibid., p. 96.

Moore cites Striedl and Ringgren as defending them.[26] In fact, Moore goes so far as to admit that "although scholars of both the present and past centuries have sometimes regarded this entire section as being independent of 1:1—9:19 and derived from a different source . . . the evidence for this is far from conclusive."[27]

30-32. And he sent letters to all the Jews, to the 127 provinces of the kingdom of Ahasuerus, namely, words of peace and truth, to establish these days of Purim at their appointed times, just as Mordecai the Jew and Queen Esther had established for them, and just as they had established for themselves and for their descendants with instructions for their times of fasting and their lamentations. And the command of Esther established these customs for Purim. Baldwin suggests that *"words of peace and truth* would be the greeting with which oriental letters began."[28] Moore finds evidence in this phrase of Esther's great caution in avoiding any appearance of hostility or imperiousness in her appeal to the minority of noncooperative Jews. But Moore goes far beyond the facts when he assumes that this residue of Jewish resistance to the correct observance of Purim continued for centuries. "Even as late as the third century A.D., however, there were still Jews who did not regard the Book of Esther as canonical."[29] This problem had nothing to do with the validity of Purim. It was caused by a lingering doubt among superstitious and legalistic Jewish minds that the book of Esther could be canonical if it did not contain the name of their God (see the Introduction).

26. Ibid., p. 95. Striedl, is Hans Striedl, "Untersuchung zur Syntax und Stilistik des hebräischen Buches Esther," *Zeitschrift für die alttestamentliche Wissenschaft* 55 (1937):73-108. Ringgren is K.V.H. Ringgren and A. Weiser, *Das Hohe Lied, Klagelieder, Das Buch Esther,* Das Alte Testament Deutsch, vol. 16, (Göttingen: Vandenhoeck & Ruprecht, 1958).
27. Moore, p. 97.
28. Baldwin, p. 420.
29. Moore, p. 96.

With instructions for their times of fasting and their lamentations reveals an additional important provision in this second official letter from Esther and Mordecai. Probably for several years now Esther and Mordecai had observed a fast on the thirteenth of Adar to commemorate the villainy of Haman (cf. 4:15-17), and probably most Jews had been doing the same thing. Therefore it was considered to be highly appropriate to establish this fast as an official day, in addition to the following two days of joy and feasting, in memory of the anxious time of fasting (and, we may be sure, of praying) that preceded God's great deliverance of His people. Such a fast may have been implied in Mordecai's first letter ("from sorrow into gladness and from mourning into a holiday" [9:22]). In any case, Jews probably began observing this fast soon after the second letter went forth, though we have no clear evidence of its observation before the ninth century after Christ. "Jews still keep this day as Esther's fast before the Purim celebrations proper, which, besides the reading of the roll of Esther in its traditional chant, accompanied by the blessings and hymns, include the festive meal and jollifications."[30]

And it was written in the book. This was not the book of Esther as such, but the book in which Mordecai had written his official record of significant events (9:20) and which doubtless served as one of the basic sources for our book of Esther.

10:1-2. Now King Ahasuerus laid a tribute on the land and on the coastlands of the sea. And all the accomplishments of his authority and strength, and the full account of the greatness of Mordecai, to which the king advanced him, are they not written in the Book of the Chronicles of the Kings of Media and Persia? In his classic *History of the Persian Empire,* A. T. Olmstead observed that "the fine promise

30. Baldwin, p. 420.

of Xerxes' younger years had not been fulfilled. Failure of the European adventure opened the way to harem intrigues, with all their deadly consequences. . . . More and more the character of Xerxes disintegrated. The enlarged but still crowded harem at Persepolis tells its own story. For a time he continued his interest in the completion of the Persepolis buildings. Toward the end of his reign, he was under the influence of the commander of the guard, the Hyrcanian Artabanus, and the eunuch chamberlain Aspamitres."[31] In 465 B.C., only eight years after the inauguration of the Feast of Purim, "Xerxes was assassinated in his bedchamer. At the head of the conspirators was Artabanus, aided by another favorite, the eunuch chamberlain Aspamitres, and by Megabyzus, the king's son-in-law, who resented the refusal of Xerxes to take action on his charge that his wife Amytis was an adulteress."[32]

The fact that the king "laid a tribute on the land and on the coastlands of the sea" in his later years (10:1) and the fact that "all the accomplishments of his authority and strength" were recorded in the official chronicles of the kingdom (10:2) do not necessarily contradict Olmstead's analysis of the moral disintegration of Xerxes (in spite of Moore's opinion)."[33] The reason for mentioning an empire-wide taxation at this point may have been to show how Xerxes prospered through Mordecai's advice to emphasize "peaceful taxation rather than plundering."[34] Because the king was, after all, "the main factor in the deliverance of the Jews,"[35] "he received his just reward, namely, a fuller treasury."[36]

---

31. A. T. Olmstead, *History of the Persian Empire* (Chicago: U. of Chicago, 1948), pp. 266-67.
32. Ibid., p. 289.
33. Moore, p. 99.
34. Ibid.
35. Jacob Hoschander, *The Book of Esther in the Light of History* (Philadelphia: Dropsie College, 1923), p. 292.
36. Moore, p. 98.

The historicity of the book of Esther is strongly asserted in verse 2 by an appeal to "the Book of the Chronicles of the Kings of Media and Persia." This formula (in its various forms) appears frequently in the books of Kings and Chronicles (e.g., 1 Kings 14:19, etc.; 2 Chron. 12:15; 13:22) and gives the clear impression that the author expected to be taken seriously, although, unfortunately, the documents cited are no longer available to us today. "The author ends his story in the same way that he began it: by speaking of the powerful and fabulous Xerxes (cf. 1:1-8 with 10:1-2). He not only cites his source of information but even invites his readers . . . to check the facts for themselves, thereby tending to establish in their minds his trustworthiness and the essential veracity of his account of Purim's origins."[37]

3. For Mordecai the Jew was second only to King Ahasuerus and great among the Jews, and in favor with the multitude of his kinsmen, one who sought the good of his people and one who spoke for the welfare of his whole nation. Mordecai's position in reference to the king reminds us again of the marvelous providence of God, who could elevate a despised Jew to a position of honor in such a fabulously wealthy and powerful empire (compare Joseph, Daniel, and Nehemiah). "The final note about Mordecai, commending his wholly good influence, is couched in thoroughly biblical terms. The prophet Zechariah says of Jerusalem's coming king, 'He shall command peace to the nations' (Zech. 9:10), and no ruler could do more than speak *peace to all his people,* even if there is a hint that Mordecai specially sought the welfare of the Jews."[38]

37. Ibid., p. 100.
38. Baldwin, p. 420.

SELECTED BIBLIOGRAPHY

Archer, Gleason L. *A Survey of Old Testament Introduction.* Rev. ed. Chicago: Moody, 1974.

Baker, Carl A. *"An Investigation of the Spirituality of Esther."* M.Div. thesis, Grace Theol. Sem., 1977.

Baldwin, J. G. "Esther." In *The New Bible Commentary: Revised,* edited by Donald Guthrie and Alec Motyer. Grand Rapids: Eerdmans, 1970.

Burn, A. R. *Persia and the Greeks: The Defense of the West 546-478 B.C.* New York: Minerva, 1968.

Coogan, Michael D. "Life in the Diaspora." *The Biblical Archaeologist* 37, no. 1 (1974):6-12.

Cumming, James E. *The Book of Esther: Its Spiritual Teaching.* London: Religious Tract Society, 1907.

Ghirshman, Roman. *The Arts of Ancient Iran.* New York: Golden, 1964.

Gordis, Robert. *Megillat Esther.* New York: Ktav, 1974.

————. "Studies in the Esther Narrative." *Journal of Biblical Literature* 95, no. 1 (March 1976):43-58.

Herodotus. *The Persian Wars.*

Hoschander, Jacob. *The Book of Esther in the Light of History.* Philadelphia: Dropsie College, 1923.

Horn, Siegfried H. "Mordecai, a Historical Problem." *Biblical Research* 9 (1964):14-25.

Hutchinson, Barbara. "An Historical Study of the Book of Esther." Research project for independent study at Ohio U. 1976.

Josephus, Flavius. *Antiquities of the Jews.*

Keil, C. F. *The Books of Ezra, Nehemiah, and Esther.* Translated by Sophia Taylor. Biblical Commentary on the Old Testament, by C. F. Keil and F. Delitzsch. 1873. Reprint. Grand Rapids: Eerdmans, 1950.

Kent, Roland G. *Old Persian.* New Haven: Am. Oriental Soc., 1953.

Littman, Robert J. "The Religious Policy of Xerxes and the Book of Esther." *The Jewish Quarterly Review,* n.s. 65, no. 3 (January 1975):145-55.

MacDonald, A. "Esther." In *The New Bible Commentary,* edited by F. Davidson. Grand Rapids: Eerdmans, 1953.

Moore, Carey A. "Archaeology and the Book of Esther." *The Biblical Archaeologist* 38, nos. 3-4 (1975):62-79.

————. *Daniel, Esther, and Jeremiah: The Additions.* The Anchor Bible. Garden City, N.Y.: Doubleday, 1977.

————. *Esther.* The Anchor Bible. Garden City, N.Y.: Doubleday, 1971.

Olmstead, A. T. *History of the Persian Empire.* Chicago: U. of Chicago, 1948.

Paton, Lewis B. *Esther.* International Critical Commentary. New York: Scribner's, 1908.

Pfeiffer, Charles F., and Vos, Howard F. *The Wycliffe Historical Geography of Bible Lands.* Chicago: Moody, 1967.

Shea, William H. "Esther and History." *Andrews University Seminary Studies* 14, no. 1 (spring 1976):227-46.

Shepperson, G. Edwin. "The Role of the Book of Esther in Salvation History." Th.M. thesis, Dallas Theol. Sem., 1975.

Urquhart, John. "Esther, Book of." In *The International Standard Bible Encyclopaedia,* 5 vols., edited by James Orr. Eerdmans, 1946, 2:1006-9.

Whitcomb, John C. *Darius the Mede.* Nutley, N.J.: Presby. & Ref., 1963.

Wood, Leon J. *A Survey of Israel's History.* Grand Rapids: Zondervan, 1970.

Wright, J. Stafford. "The Historicity of Esther." In *New Perspectives on the Old Testament,* edited by J. Barton Payne, pp. 37-47. Waco, Tex.: Word, 1970.

Yamauchi, Edwin M. "The Achaemenid Capitals." *Near East Archaeology Society Bulletin,* n.s. no. 8 (1976):5-81.

Young, Edward J. *An Introduction to the Old Testament.* Grand Rapids: Eerdmans, 1949.